The Gauntlet *of* Grief

CHRIS SPAIN

ISBN 978-1-63784-203-4 (paperback)
ISBN 978-1-63784-204-1 (digital)

Hawes & Jenkins Publishing
16427 N Scottsdale Road Suite 410
Scottsdale, AZ 85254
www.hawesjenkins.com

Printed in the United States of America

Contents

The Plan?

ost people have a plan until they get hit. Mine came over the Christmas holidays in 2013. I was going through a divorce, my second, and it was a pretty nasty one at that. My Christian walk was all but destroyed. I had no job or money; I had no plan. I had moved back to Alabama from Mississippi. I was starting over with the clothes on my back. The only blessing that I could see in this was my kids. At least, I had them. I have had custody of them since they were four and five years old. Their names were Peyton and Erin.

My sister (Sandy) and brother-in-law (Johnny) were gracious enough to bring us into their home. All that my kids wanted to do was play soccer. Sandy's home was zoned for Hueytown High School, and they had just started a soccer program there. Finally, I caught a break. They actually were getting to do what they truly desired. The only catch to living with my sister was that they had to start attending church. It was a house rule. They were saved, but their walk was almost nonexistent. They were not happy about it at first, but quickly changed when they got plugged into the youth group. I am so grateful to Sandy and Johnny, just for that alone.

During the Christmas holidays, the kids went on a church trip to the mountains to snow ski. The busyness of my life had slowed down, and I was alone—defeated. I had no clue what to do next. I began to cry because I felt that my life was a wreck. There have been so many tribulations in my life. An unmistakable pain shot through my chest. Was it a heart attack? Is it finally coming to a close for me? As these thoughts ran through my head, a peace covered me like a warm blanket. That was it: "So, because you are lukewarm—neither hot nor cold—I am about to spit you out of my mouth" (Revelations 3:16 NIV). I felt like God was trying to get my attention. I had been spit out, but God sucked me back in. Here is the moment. I was lukewarm. Was I really going to believe in this God stuff or not? God has been with me. I knew him. It was just that every time I failed, I would lose a little more faith. Am I going hot or cold? Well, I am here to tell you that I made the right choice.

After that day, things started getting better. They were not good, mind you. I just had a little more positive outlook. Let there be no mistake. It was God. In a few days, He brought me back together with an old high school friend. You guessed it, through Facebook. I started a Facebook page because I know social media is looked at by employers. It wasn't but a few days until Tracie hit me up. "My Chris!" was typed on my wall. We dated briefly in high school, but we stayed pretty good friends. Well, as I was staring at the computer, all I could think about was anger, divorce, and having nothing. (Sorry, ladies, but I didn't like you very much.) You guessed it. I blew her off. She got a cookie-cutter response that said that I'm just going through a bad patch, and it was good to hear from her. God was adding her to my life for a reason. She didn't bite, and I'm grateful. Over the next few weeks, we talked, and I felt like we had a "feel sorry for me" competition at times. We talked like that twenty-five-year gap was not there. Her seventeen-year marriage had just ended. She was hungry for the Word, and so was I. We read scripture to each other almost every night. God had a plan. We just had no clue what it was. The kids got involved, and we started hanging out pretty often as a group. Her kids and mine melded pretty quickly. The kids and I were standoffish, but I knew God was in it.

Then, God laid a specific scripture on us. It was Matthew 7:3–5, which says, "Why do you look at the speck of sawdust in your brother's eye and pay no attention to the plank in your own eye? How can you say to your brother, 'Let me take the speck out of your eye,' when all of the time there is a plank in your own eye?' You hypocrite, first take the plank out of your own eye, and you will see clearly to remove the speck from your own brother's eye." Tracie always called it "the plank, speck, eyeball thingy." He kept us in that scripture for over two months. Every time we tried to read another scripture, we wound up back there. It was so weird, but let me show you what came from it.

Remember, I have two failed marriages, right? See, I only included God in my personal life as well as my home, but I never submitted to Him. All this did was give Him a front-row seat to the destruction of marriages. Now I can go on for days, but the image that I want to plant in your head is that I put God in a chair, chained Him up, and made Him watch us drive our marriages into the ground. Then I would toss Him a key so He could unlock Himself and clean it up. It doesn't make much sense, does it? After all, I was the kids' baseball coach or soccer coach. You know, whatever season was going on, I was in it. We just didn't have time to read the Bible or go to church often. Sunday was a day of rest, right? You get the idea. Before this scripture, it was really easy to blame the ex-wives. We all get self-involved, and it is easy to take our eyes off what God has bestowed on us.

I had an inner circle of friends to which Tracie was added. I have known these friends for many years. I met Jennifer in junior high school. I think our friendship really flourished in high school when we were assigned lockers next to each other. Jennifer was a cheerleader, and I was a football player. I have to admit that I started talking to Jennifer because she was pretty. I was a teenage boy full of hormones, so you get the idea. My plan was to wait out her boyfriend and then ask her out. Thirty years later, they're married, and I'm still trying to wait him out. In all seriousness, Jennifer and her husband, Keith, have been close friends of mine. I've worked with Jennifer, and our kids played together as far back as when they were in diapers. Radar was added to my life just after high school. We went to junior high and high school together but were in different cliques of friends. I think our bond really started because of our mutual interest in billiards. Out of my group, my relationship with Radar has been the closest. Andy was added to my group shortly after Radar. Andy was going through a terrible time in his life with the death of his father and started hanging out with us because his brother was friends with Radar. At the beginning, he was more of a tagalong. Our bond got closer as time went on, especially during football season. There were several friends in our group at that time, but Radar and Andy adhered to me more through the years. Kevin was probably the newest of my friends. I met him when I moved to Mississippi. I immediately had tremendous respect for him because he had started the Boys and Girls Club in that area and had a tremendous passion for kids. He coached ball teams and mentored hundreds of kids in our county. The amazing part of this is that he put this passion in front of his own personal desires for a family. Character counts, and I saw his right off the bat. These people became more than friends to me. Each of them is more like a brother or a sister. This family of friends later became my hedge of protection.

Things were rocking along pretty well. Tracie, the kids, and I would hang out with Andy at Radar's. From time to time, Tracie would go with us to see Kevin or Jennifer. All of us are believers, so we would all get into scripture on occasion.

The soccer season came and went. It was their first year, so I'll save you from that repetitive beating. The important part of it was the new friendships that both Peyton and Erin made, as well as me. It was like they had two sets of friends that they both wanted to bring into one group. One was church, and the other was soccer. They couldn't quite manage to get them together. It was okay though. They were true to both sets. Peyton would just hang out with whichever group gathered, while Erin took more of my high school approach. She wasn't snobby. She was busy. The focus was always on what she was doing. It wasn't about who it was with. She had her church friends, then had soccer friends during the seasons.

They both started really enjoying life again. That is, until the youth minister left abruptly. They didn't get to say goodbye. I remember a bull session we had about it a few weeks later. Peyton, with tears in his eyes, asked if I had heard the rumor that was going around about the youth minister that left. I told him that I had heard it, too, but it didn't matter to me. Peyton was defensive and quite angry about this rumor, I might add. Both of the kids cared a great deal for this man. They said that he actually was interested in their lives. He didn't put on a show. This is where God is awesome! I got to really show them the meaning of the "plank, speck, eyeball thingy." I used scripture to ease their pain. It didn't matter what mistakes he may have made. He was a man who made mistakes, like all of us in times of weakness. He changed their walks. That was what mattered, and I am grateful for that, too.

Do to others as you would have them do to you.

(LUKE 6:31 NIV)

The Way Home

D o you know where you were on April 6, 2015? I will never
forget it. I was on my way home from North Alabama and
decided to stop and eat with Tracie. As we were finishing
our meal, Peyton's girlfriend called me. She simply asked if I knew
where the kids were. I looked at my phone and told her that they
should be on their way home from soccer practice. That was when
she informed me that they had been in a wreck. I don't know how
she knew about the accident so quickly, but that is how I found out.
As I learned information about the circumstances of the accident,
I quickly relayed them to Sandy. I sent Sandy to the hospital to be
with one of my children—which I later found out to be Peyton—
while I investigated the whereabouts of the other one. As I headed
to Birmingham with Tracie following me, I called Radar to meet me
at the convenience store by his house just off the interstate. Tracie,
Radar, his family, and I spent the next hour in the parking lot trying
to uncover where my daughter was. I must have called 911 a dozen
times to no avail. At the end of that hour, Sandy called me and let me
know that the police had gone to the house and notified my nephew
that Erin had died at the scene. She also let me know that Peyton

was in emergency surgery and that they had removed one kidney and his spleen. This was when I realized how dire the situation was. For the hospital to do surgery without my permission, it had to be life and death. Tracie drove me to the hospital while Radar took my truck back home. On the way to the hospital, I finally received a call directly from the coroner. When he informed me that Erin had passed away, I asked to go see her. He told me that there was nothing I could do for her and I should continue to go to the hospital because my son was fighting for his life. Shock had completely come over me. I had no idea what to do next.

When we got to Birmingham, we went into three parking lots before we got to the correct spot where Peyton's girlfriend was waiting for us. She escorted us to the waiting area where what seemed like half of Hueytown High School was waiting. I was taken to a conference area where I joined my dad, two sisters with their families respectively, and the staff of First Baptist Church Pleasant Grove (FBCPG). This was the point that I found out how serious of a condition Peyton was in. I remember they told me he had just gotten out of emergency surgery. They had to interrupt the surgery and call off because he was bleeding out. At this time, he was in radiology having a CT scan. I remember hitting my knees; my prayer was simple: "Lord, you have my daughter. Please don't take my son. Just leave me one." God was silent. It seemed like just moments had passed when the neurosurgeon came in. When he locked eyes with me and realized I was the father, his bottom lip started quivering. I knew. An unmistakable pain pierced my heart. He quickly let me know that he was a resident but had conferred with the chief of neurosurgery. Both of them had reviewed the scans and concurred. He said that Peyton had gone without oxygen and blood to his brain for too long. Then he said there was no hope. I looked into his eyes and asked him if he was sure that there was no hope. As tears welled in his eyes, he said, "No." I remember being calm, saying, "Thank you," and asked when I could see him. He told me that he was being transported from radiology and that someone would come get me as soon as he got to his room. It seems like time passed very quickly. There were several pastors that converged on me and began to pray.

Before I knew it, I was taken to Peyton's room. When I walked in, he was on a ventilator. Sheets covered his entire body up to his neck. He had a black eye and a few scratches on his forehead. Even with the ventilator, his breathing was not solid. It was like he had a hiccup when he exhaled. I spent a few minutes praying over him, and a peace came over me. I knew in my heart that he was gone. God let me know.

I left Peyton's room and headed back to the waiting room. I remember the associate pastor of FBCPG stopping me. He asked me where I was going. I turned and told him that I have a hundred and fifty people in the waiting room that needed to know. I remember him specifically telling me to stop because we needed a plan. I waited a few minutes for him while he gathered the rest of his staff. We went into the waiting room as a group, and I broke the news to all of Peyton's friends. As people broke down and cried, the church staff started ministering to the people. The church staff was in transition, so they had both the old staff and the interim staff at the hospital. I remember saying that they were in interim for this very reason. Again, this was part of His plan. As I finished, I told everyone that if they wanted to see Peyton before his body passed away, this would be the time. I saw something then that showed me God was in the middle of it. Johnny (my brother-in-law) took teenaged kids in groups to see Peyton. As he carried them back there, he professed Christ to them. Can you imagine? He put his grief aside to seek the opportunity to try to bring Christ to their lives.

While I was talking to everyone in the hospital waiting room, God was setting His plan in motion. I was so numb that I could not think of how to put one step in front of the other. Tracie had made contact with friends and family to get the news out. It seemed that within minutes, I was talking to the people that God placed in my life to protect me. Kevin had to make the trip from Mississippi, and Andy was at work, so I physically did not see them until the next morning. Jennifer was added to Tracie and Radar that night at the hospital. These three of my hedge of five helped me get through the worst night of my life.

It seemed as if the groups of teenagers finished seeing Peyton at about 1:30 that morning. That is when I went back to see him again. I sat by his bed and prayed. Tears started coming from his eyes, and his arm moved. I got up and got the nurse. As she was checking him, his blood pressure went through the roof. It stayed high momentarily and then started dropping to nothing. This was it. His body was leaving. The doctor on the floor ran to me and asked what she should do. As I said previously, the Lord had laid it on my heart that he was gone. I told her, "Do not resuscitate. Let him go." That is when the counselor from the Alabama Organ Center came to me. She asked me if I knew what his change in blood pressure meant. I told her that I did. She then asked me if she could get the doctors to give Peyton medication while we had a minute to talk. I told her that was fine. They gave him medicine to stabilize his vitals, and she took me back to the conference room. It did not take but just a couple of minutes to realize what she was asking of me. She navigated the field of organ donation with great sensitivity and knowledge. As soon as she could get my mind back to the reality of what was happening, it was a no-brainer to tell her to proceed.

Consider it pure joy, my brothers and sisters,
whenever you face trials of many kinds,
because you know that the testing of your
faith produces perseverance. Let perseverance
finish its work so that you may be mature
and complete, not lacking anything.

(JAMES 1:2–4 NIV)

Fight with Love?

The longest forty-eight hours of my life are coming next. They stabilized Peyton's blood pressure and began donor matches. As that was going on, I hit my knees again. I did not ask God why. I did not get angry. I only had one simple question: What now, God? What do I do now? For the first time, I heard God respond to me in an audible voice. He told me very clearly to obey Him and to fight with love. To be quite honest, I did not know what to do with that, so I went to Radar. Radar has been a mentor to me in the Bible and one of my best friends for over twenty years. I think it's easy to say that God stumped us both that night. The next few days, God showed me exactly what He meant by that. The rest of that night was somewhat uneventful. Friends were coming from out of town, donor matching was going on, and I was just trying to wrap my head around what was happening. I wound up spending most of that morning in the parking deck with my friends trying to figure out what to do next. I knew I couldn't leave the hospital but knew my daughter was only a block away in the county morgue. My friends changed gears and started to protect me and take care of me. I think I ate twice that morning by eight o'clock.

When the world started operating again the next morning, I made my phone calls to see Erin. I was informed that there was no way I could see her because there were other bodies there and they had no place to set up visitation for me. I remember looking at Radar and making a statement that he would later use against me for the next few months. "I am angered by the fact that government bureaucracy is impeding my grief." I know that sounds weird, but Radar used that statement to make sure that I did not hinder anyone else's grief process through this dark time. As we were standing there talking, all I could think of was anger. My son's gone. I watched him pass before my very eyes. Now they won't let me see my daughter. Remember what God spoke to me? Here was my first challenge to fight with love. This tragedy was all over the news. People were contacting me from all over. It would be very easy to put ungodly pressure on the people of Jefferson County. I mean, they couldn't even put Erin into a room at the county morgue just for me to see her for a few minutes? Really? And then that wave of peace came again. Fight with love. I contacted the coroner's office and let them know how disappointed I was. They in turn let me know the exact process that I had to go through in order to see Erin as soon as possible. We've all dealt with government bureaucracy. Empathy is not a government machine's strong point, so fighting with anger would have been futile.

By this time, midmorning, I had eaten three times, and the second wave of my hedge had arrived and were there. The full complement of five had now completely surrounded me. Kevin, Andy, and Jennifer were now there to give Tracie and Radar a much-needed break. I don't know what goes through people's minds when you're in the middle of a disaster like this, but I believe they were truly concerned about my well-being. "Geez." I couldn't even go to the bathroom by myself. Let there be no mistake, I am very grateful for them. I don't know what I would have done without these friends. I believe that they truly saved my life. Not only did they counsel, but they gave godly counsel. God was doing a work in us all.

The counselor from the Alabama Organ Center tracked me down. By this time, they had a good grasp of the schedule for Peyton's donation. She informed me that tissue and bone donation was impossible due to the number of blood transfusions he had to have. There were no donations able to be given from anything in his head due to the trauma from the wreck. The pancreas was not available because they had to remove the spleen. One of his kidneys was removed in surgery, so it was unavailable. Donor matching was found for a heart recipient, liver recipient, and one kidney recipient. They had a backup recipient for his lung even though they were doubtful that this gift would be salvageable as well. This was a very trying moment. No matter how well the counselor was able to give me this information, we were still talking about my son. It was like having a knife thrust into your chest all over again. I asked her when this procedure would take place. Her response was this evening. This was the point that I changed modes to just trying to get through it.

The Lord is closer to the broken hearted
and saves those who are crushed in spirit.

(PSALMS 34:18 NIV)

"Just Pick One, Dad"

My sister called me again to talk about funeral homes. I had no clue what to do next. I remember sitting in the parking deck of the hospital crying. I could not seem to gather the strength to get out of the car. Enormous grief had overtaken me along with starting to worry about the financial side of this. It wasn't but just a few minutes that I received a phone call. One of the soccer moms on Erin's team decided to put a GoFundMe account together. I saw very quickly why my hedge included women. Between Tracie, my sister, and this soccer mom, a GoFundMe account was put together in a matter of hours. I did not have life insurance on the kids. I did not have much money in the bank. I felt as if I had nothing. I would not be able to finish taking care of the kids. The word spread quickly about the GoFundMe account, and donations came in from all over the country. Donations were made from as far as New York to Montana to Texas. People donated to my cause when they didn't even know me. What a blessing God bestowed on me just in that alone.

The generosity kept on coming. My dad and stepmom offered up their burial plots in their hometown. At the same time, burial plots were donated to me closer to home. What I did not realize was that God was tapping people to take care of my every need. My sister took the lead and started the process of contacting the funeral home and making arrangements.

By now, my hedge of protection was in full motion. Accounts were set up, financial transactions were being monitored, and people known throughout our lives were being contacted. It was like this process was back on track. That is when the counselor contacted me again. She let me know that Peyton's operation was going to be postponed to the next morning. This gave me the ability to spend the afternoon setting up funeral arrangements.

I have now eaten five times today. My hedge has decided that I am not to be left alone for any reason at any time. It's not because of anything I'm saying that may be mistaken for suicidal thoughts or behavior; it is simply because the reality of this has now sunk in. Kevin and Radar are now on each side of me demanding toilet paper as proof that I really went to the bathroom because I put my foot down and said I would go to the bathroom alone. I think it was the first time that I saw us laugh when Kevin actually asked for toilet paper.

Jennifer pulled me to the side and let me know that she had talked to Sandy. The funeral home needed my signatures for the releases to pick up the kids' bodies. I had to physically leave the hospital for the first time. My hedge consisted of three men, all weighing 300 pounds or better, and two beautiful women. Let there be no mistake, Jennifer is the toughest in the group. When something needed to be done, she was the one that made me do it. She had to make me leave the hospital that day to take care of matters at the funeral home. We all took separate cars to the convenience store up the street from the funeral home. I believe I rode with Andy there. We parked three cars and all got into one and continued our journey to the cemetery.

When we got to the funeral home, I met the funeral director. This is where my experience differed from anyone I have spoken to. The funeral director put me under his wing and told me that he was going to treat me like his son.

"Thank you for that, Charlie." If I began to spend too much money, he was going to reel me in. We started out by signing the documents I needed to sign, and we quickly moved to the caskets. Going into that room was mortifying. There were caskets lined up from wall to wall. Sandy and Johnny were the only two in there with me and the funeral director. This is where I felt the spirit of the kids with me for the first time. Erin's voice kept reverberating in my head that this was pretty and that was ugly and don't do this and do that. It took us about three or four minutes before we came upon Erin's casket. It was a beautiful teal color, lined with gold. I was still worried about finances, so I was very price conscious when we were there. Even though this casket had gold accents all over it, the price was reasonable, so I settled on that one for her. Peyton's voice started reverberating in my head when we started searching for his.

I kept hearing, "Oh my gosh, Dad, just pick one. You know I don't care!" There was a beautiful crimson casket on the back wall, but it was a thousand dollars more. After a minute or two of thought, I decided the kids needed matching caskets. It was settled. Both of my kids were to be buried in these beautiful teal and gold caskets. We then went back into the conference room and discussed funeral arrangements. This was when the realization of the kids' impact on the community hit. They were concerned about dealing with crowd control. That is when Johnny spoke up and said the church would handle it. They had security for matters such as this as well as media control measures. They were also large enough to handle two funerals of this capacity. When all of this was settled, we headed outside to pick out the burial spots. I will never forget the moment that we picked them out. Sandy asked about having a bench. I told Sandy that there are some things that I care about, but this wasn't one of them. She needed to take the reins and pick out whatever she wanted. She pointed to a bench and said, "I want this bench."

I just smiled and said, "It looks like we're going to have an India red bench to sit on beside the kids," and she smiled.

We were out by the house, so this was a good time to take a shower and reset before going to the hospital. We all gathered around and freshened up before we headed back. There was food brought in for us if needed, and my hedge would not let me leave without eating.

I have now eaten six times today, and I'm heading back to the hospital. When I got there, I went straight back to Peyton and asked the nurse if there was any change. Unfortunately, she said no. I visited with him and prayed for about an hour. As I came out, my hedge had procured a spot in the back of the waiting room. Jennifer told me that I would get some rest either by choice or after she had knocked me out. I knew I wouldn't be able to sleep, but I had to try. The end of day two was coming, and everyone was exhausted.

Should we accept only good things from
the hand of God and never anything bad?

(JOB 2:10B NLV)

Teal or Crimson?

I got up at about 2:30 that morning. Four hours of broken sleep was all that I could muster. My ritual was to go see Peyton, and Kevin was my bodyguard on that shift. After spending a couple of hours with Peyton, the counselor let me know that the operation was moved back to 7:00 a.m. The heart transplant recipient was going through health complications, and they were trying to stabilize him. All that could go through my head was "this was a mistake." I cannot get closure, and this is going to linger on forever. Kevin and I went down to see if the cafeteria was open because I had not eaten yet at 4:30 a.m. The cafeteria did not open until 5:30, so I had an hour to kill. Kevin and I went out in the parking lot and reminisced about the kids and his involvement in their lives. Again, the process seemed to get back on track. We went to eat as the doors opened to the cafeteria because, you know, I was wasting away. After eating, I bought Radar some fruit—the breakfast of champions—and we went upstairs to wake him up. I had a question for him, and I felt like it was time-sensitive. The three of us had a brief discussion about my thoughts on both ex-wives being present at the kids' funeral. I asked Radar for his thoughts. He responded with one question, "Do you want to become the bureaucracy that impedes others' grief?" This discussion stopped because I realized it was a quarter to seven and the transplant operation was just a few minutes away. This was heavy on my heart, and I had a feeling God was not going to let it go, but there was no time to deal with it now. The counselor came to me and said there was another delay. It was going to be noon before the operation was going to begin. We contacted family and friends to let them know of the delay. Five more hours of this grueling hell was to take place.

At about nine o'clock, Radar looked at the GoFundMe account and let me know that there was enough money in that account to now pay for the funerals. I know that this may seem strange, but there was a weight taken off me. It's like their first school supply run, registration, and school clothes. When they are registered and everything is paid, relief comes over you. Well, that's how it felt. I can finish this. Then, Tracie relayed a phone conversation between her and Sandy. Let me preface this with the understanding that Johnny is one of the biggest Auburn fans that you will ever meet. So she let me know that it was laid on Johnny's heart that Peyton should be buried in the crimson casket that we had looked at because Peyton was a pretty big Bama fan, too. It was about one thousand more dollars, so originally, I passed. Now, I had the money. He was going to be buried in the crimson casket, and she was going to be buried in the teal casket.

It is now 10:30 in the morning. I have eaten twice today, and I am headed back to Peyton's room. As I began to pray, God laid on my heart a scripture to read. The scripture that was laid on my heart to read was Matthew 5:3, the opening verse of the Sermon on the Mount and the section of the sermon known as the Beatitudes. I sent Tracie to get my Bible. After a few minutes, she came back, and we sat down together and read the scripture. I didn't really know where to stop, just where to begin, so I repeatedly read to Peyton Matthew 5:3–16. As I was reading through it for the third time with eyes full of tears, Peyton's maternal grandparents came into the room. I stopped in the middle of scripture and greeted them and told them to wait just a moment. I finished reading the scripture and then spoke to them. This is when I remember Radar using my words against me—don't let bureaucracy impede others' grief. When I greeted them, I let them know that the operation was about to take place. God laid it on my heart to give them some time alone with Peyton. Tracie and I stepped out of the room and talked to the counselor, once again concerned that I was going to give up my last moments with my son. She just gently placed her hand on my shoulder and said that they would not start without me. If this ran a little long, everyone could wait for fifteen more minutes.

Everyone got to say their goodbyes, and the nurse asked me how I would like to proceed with the last moment that I could spend with him. She told me that the end of my walk with him would be at the elevators. I told her that I would walk to the elevators, but when they opened for them to go in and go down, "Do not stop. Do not pause for me." That is pretty much what happened. I turned around to Tracie and told her it was over. She had my Bible in one hand, my drink in another, and a bag of belongings of some sort in her arms. I could not bear to stand in a cold elevator hallway to say goodbye, so I did it in the room before they escorted him out.

When the surgery began, I just asked to be let known when it was over. Three and a half hours later, after sitting in another waiting room, I got the word that it was done. There was indescribable grief and an incredible peace that hit me at the same time. I was then able to leave.

Look at the birds of the air; they do not
sow or reap or store away in barns and yet
your heavenly father feeds them. Are you
not much more valuable than they?

(MATTHEW 6:26 NIV)

My Angel

We are finally leaving the hospital, and there is no word on Erin. The process was under way to get her to the funeral home and start preparations for the funeral, but there was no word on whether or not she had been transported at this time. To be honest, I don't remember if my hedge even told me that I could see Erin or not and that she had arrived. We were on our way to the funeral home before I knew it. The entourage of vehicles looked like the president was on his way. There must have been five or six cars lined up. We got to the funeral home, and I was informed that they had done just enough to basically clean Erin up so I could see her. It is Wednesday afternoon, and I had not seen her for a couple of days now. They escorted us into a room, and she was on a table. Her hair was still wet from a bath, and she was covered with a velvet blanket up to her neck. I lost it. I began to cry uncontrollably—you know what I mean, one of those ugly cries. I yelled, "Oh my baby," as I ran to her and hugged her. She was cold—lifeless. Her eyes were closed, and she had a small cut on her right cheek. The cut was unnoticeable to most, but I could see it. She looked like an angel. As I was over her, all I could think of was, *Why can't you hug me back?*

The realization that she was gone had hit. I turned back around and saw my family and friends just staring at me. There were no words. It was a moment that I will never forget, and I pray that many will not have to go through.

I had to reset. I had to regain my composure, so I walked outside. I can't remember exactly who was with me when I walked outside, but I know I wasn't alone. This is when the funeral director summoned me to him. He sat me down in the foyer and began to tell me other things that were transpiring. He let me know that the kids' birth mother and stepmother had contacted him. They had attempted to change the obituary and procure the kids' bodies to have their own service. I was speechless. What do you say to that? I had just finally seen my baby girl after walking through my other baby's body being donated, and here comes drama. I looked at Charlie and asked him what his response was and what he did. We had to get into some legalistic issues for a moment. I don't remember specifically if I had to show him my divorce decree where I had full custody of the kids or if he just took my word for it. He informed me that he was going to do so according to my wishes. I let him know that I needed to wrap my head around this for a moment before I could tell him how to proceed. The standing orders to him were to continue as planned until he heard from me. At this point, I had not decided anything—whether to have visitation that night, the next day, funeral time, or anything else dealing with the funeral. Remember, Peyton's body had to go to the morgue before going to the funeral home, and my babies are still not together. I know that when I walked outside after this meeting, Charlie spoke to my brother-in-law in more detail about what was going on. As I was outside, the words reverberated in my head over and over and over "fight with love." We put it to the side for now so my family could spend ten or fifteen minutes with my child. This was something that was going to have to be addressed, but I couldn't deal with it right now. I didn't need this. After all, who needs ex-wife drama when you're having to set up arrangements for the burial of your kids?

You are altogether beautiful, my
darling; there is no flaw in you.

(SONG OF SOLOMON 4:7 NIV)

Love, Fried Chicken,
and Sledgehammers

We dispersed from the funeral home. When everyone met at the house, it reminded me of a holiday. There were people throughout the house—some friends, some family. They were all in small groups around the house talking. Some were talking; some were reheating food that was brought from Sandy's Sunday school class. Yes, you guessed it. I was about to eat for the fourth time today, and there were all types of food there. I remember there was fried chicken, casseroles, desserts, and just about anything you could think of. The church again showed their love.

When the evening started slowing down, it was time to address what had happened at the funeral home earlier that day. The consensus of the group was not only to ban the ex-wives from the funeral, but to prevent them from being in Pleasant Grove altogether. I just did not need this drama added to this day. I remember telling the group that this didn't feel right and I needed a minute to step outside. On the back porch, I must have walked a mile talking to God without moving twenty feet. Everyone has a plan until they get hit, remember? Right now, it feels like a 20-pound sledgehammer hitting me over the head. It felt like God was walking those paces with me. In fact, I have seen on television where disaster victims have blankets wrapped around them with someone consoling them. This is how I sensed God being with me. His blanket of love was wrapped around me. I knew what to do. I was not happy about it, and I knew the people inside wouldn't be happy about it either, but this is what God wanted. A compromise was coming. I was not going to impede someone else's grieving process. It was not going to happen. I went back inside and told the group what God had laid on my heart. I believe it was the first time that anyone actually heard what God had laid on me to do from the beginning, with the exception of Radar. "Be obedient and fight with love." As I let the group know, I saw the anger on their faces relent. It was like God put a peace on their hearts as well. We weren't completely sure what the compromise was going to be yet because we had not actually talked specifically about the funeral schedule. Sandy worked repeatedly on me to help me realize that a viewing on Friday night and a funeral on Saturday would probably be more than I could bear. It made sense. Saturday would be a gauntlet day, but it would be over in one day. Now that I know that I'm going to do a one-day service, how do I compromise for the ex-wives and their families to have their time? The decisions seemed to come very easily. God was in it. The funeral director had told us that the kids would be at the church by eight o'clock regardless of when we decided to start the service. That's when I decided to give them the first hour. They could have an hour to do what they wanted, and then we would start the day at nine.

My command is this: Love each
other as I have loved you.

(JOHN 15:12 NIV)

A Community
Coming Together

Thursday morning was another day of torture for me, even though nothing major went on for me personally. It was more about getting the ball rolling on the funeral arrangements. When I woke up, there were breakfast casseroles all over the kitchen, so of course, I ate.

The decision was made in the hospital for my stepmom to write the obituaries, and it had already been done by this time. I vaguely remembered it, other than thinking that my stepmom would be the perfect person for it because of her background in administration. The maternal grandparents owned a printshop and offered to help with programs and decals that were made. Sandy handled that with them, and it all worked out beautifully. I remember the programs were being dealt with that morning alongside letting the world know the times of the funerals. My hedge as well as my family were in full swing. Johnny was the unfortunate one that was tapped to notify the ex-wives of when their viewing time would be. I was sent to the Galleria to pick out a suit. Yep, the one that I would wear to bury the kids in. Before I left, I had to make sure that I had eaten because, you know, it would be a couple of hours before I got back.

How do you pick out what you are going to wear on a day like this? I am so glad, again, that my hedge included women. If it were left up to me and the guys, I probably would have been in a T-shirt and shorts. Seriously though, we shopped and found a nice suit with a tie that matched Peyton and Erin. I had decided to bury them in their Easter outfits from the previous year. It took us a couple of hours to find that suit. Quite frankly, I'm an odd size, and my measurements are not readily available. I'm a 31" length in pants—not a 30" or 32"". I wear a 42R jacket, but the sleeves are a half inch too long. My shirt size is an XL, but I have an 18 ½" neck due to my high school wrestling career. So as you see, once I found a suit, I could not find a shirt that would match, or I would only find part of a suit without the other part. We had two days before the funeral, so alterations at the store were not possible. Sandy called a woman in her Sunday school class who agreed to take care of my suit that night. This is just another of many examples where God was in it, taking care of my needs.

By the time we got home that afternoon, another wave of food had arrived. Just on a side note, if you have a hedge of protection, make sure they talk to each other about eating schedules for you because, you guessed it, I needed to eat. People were coming in by groups that evening. Friends of mine, friends of Sandy and Johnny, as well as friends of the kids were making their way to the house.

That evening was so bittersweet. We talked about the kids as if they were with us. The evening was spent sitting around throughout the house. We were laughing and crying. Some of us were sitting on the front porch when one specific conversation started with the interim youth pastor's wife. She just looked at me and said that my son was so sweet. My response to her was "you sure that's my kid you're talking about?" I remember the look on her face. It changed to the expression of "okay I have to be honest."

"Your son was a turd. Just a turd!"

We all busted out laughing, and I said, "Yep, that's my P-Man." Peyton loved aggravating people. He was a chip off the old block. I began telling her about a joke we had been playing on each other. We flipped the front tags on each other's vehicles upside down. It went on for months. Tracie believes she started it, but I'm pretty sure that Peyton finished it. Stories like this went on all night. I have no idea what time it was when we turned in for the evening, but everyone made sure that I ate one more time.

The next morning had already been set up, and my first activity of the day was to go to the high school. On the way to the school, we decided to drive by the crash site. It was the first time we had been by there. The road they crashed on was a small two-lane road that cut over to the high school. It was pretty well traveled but not a major throughway. Just a matter of feet from the crash site was a man. He had his thumb out as if he was hitching a ride. I remember Kevin saying that we had a woman in the car, so he was not going to stop. Let me iterate. This man was standing beside a bridge on a road in the middle of the woods. He was very well-dressed and clean-cut. It was the oddest sight I think I had ever seen. Although we did not stop, we made phone calls and sent the man some help. It was just a few minutes before someone got to the area where the man was standing, and he had disappeared. Parts of me regret not stopping, but I felt in the same breath that I wasn't supposed to stop. I'm still trying to figure out what that was about.

We continued to make our way to the high school for a meeting at nine with the administration. We had gotten very close to the assistant principal at the school. She looked after the kids a little more than she actually had to. She was instrumental in getting the soccer program on its feet from the beginning. Even though she was in administration, she helped the kids on and off the field. We instantly loved her. I was drawn to let her know the events that had happened in detail because I felt as though she was more like family. We started the meeting with me giving her an organ donor family pin to wear at the funeral, and I handed out donor bracelets to everyone at the table. I had no idea of the surprises that were awaiting me as well. She responded in kind with an envelope where they had taken up a donation for me. From there, I gave her the detailed events that went on with Peyton's organ donation. I think it would be sufficient to say that there was not a dry eye in the room. It was a very difficult meeting to get through. She let me know that I wasn't alone in my pain. She wanted to show me what the student body was doing to work out their grief as well. We went as a group to each of the kids' lockers. The posters, sticky notes, and flowers that were taped on their lockers completely enveloped them. I didn't cry; I was in awe. My kids impacted this school much greater than I realized. After we finished the lockers in the main school, we moved on to Erin's gym locker. We got a giggle out of the fact that this was a brand-new school and kids had written with a sharpie all over her locker door. The administrators just had a confused look on their faces. You could tell they had no clue how to deal with this love/vandalism. I did not envy them. From there, we finished up by going by the front office and collecting their belongings. As we were walking to our car, it was pointed out to us that Peyton's parking spot had also been decorated by the students with sidewalk chalk and flowers. Everyone reserved that spot for him for the rest of the school year. Another bittersweet moment for which I'm grateful.

The afternoon was spent giving last-minute instructions to Brother Daven Watkins (the preacher that would perform the service), making sure that the former youth minister was going to be able to come, and making sure that the pall bearers were set. You know, just getting the details finalized. The rest of the evening was another night like the previous. Friends and family were gathered around talking and carrying on with memories of the kids. Gatlin, Peyton's best friend from Mississippi, was in town, and my mom was there, so we were ready.

The king will reply, Truly I tell you, whatever
you did for one of the least of these brothers
and sisters of mine, you did for me.

(MATTHEW 25:40)

Just Breathe!

pril 11, 2015, Saturday, is the day that I will never forget. As I woke up, a heaviness was on me that I cannot describe. The morning started off with prayer. I knew each step was going to get heavier and it was going to hurt more as I went, but I had one job: Get this done and survive it. That morning, both ex-wives were already having their moments with the kids when we started getting ready. There was one little thing that we had to do first though. It was my sister's birthday. Although I knew that there was no choice, the full weight of this hit me. I'm burying my kids on Sandy's birthday. Again, I'm grateful that my hedge included women. Jennifer and Tracie had put a gift basket together for Sandy. It had massage oils in it, lotions, aromatherapy items, and a gift certificate for a massage. So this is how the morning started. I know Sandy's birthday had to have been miserable, but she handled it like a trooper. We were downstairs, and we had just given her the basket. I looked around, and yep, you guess it, I needed to eat again. I can't remember what I ate that morning, but I know I picked through several different things, between breakfast casseroles, biscuits, and sausage. It was basically a buffet that morning. It had to be though because I bet there were a dozen people there. Everyone ate, but I don't remember much conversation going on. It was serious, and everyone was just trying to get the day started.

I remember loading up in Tracie's car, but for the life of me, I cannot remember who drove. It didn't matter though. Everyone was focused on what was coming. As we got there, the church had everything set up to the last detail. I did not have to make any decisions, and I was escorted everywhere we went. Security was tight. I believe there were twenty off-duty police officers around the campus. The first place we went was straight to where the kids were in the sanctuary. Erin was so beautiful. She was at peace. Peyton was still scratched up and scuffed up a little bit more than I would have liked, but still a very handsome young man. Peyton's girlfriend made me aware that his bow tie was upside down. Tracie was sent to deal with that. I walked up and down the sanctuary looking at the flowers and all the pictures around the room. That is when it hit me—both of my kids were gone. Whom am I going to stand by? Another detail God had already worked out. If you remember, I spent three days in the hospital with Peyton. It was Erin that I couldn't see. So my place was set. I stood by my daughter on her day of rest. It didn't seem like it, but it was just a few minutes when they were escorting people through the doors. I don't know how many people I saw that day, but it seemed like a never-ending line. I greeted friends and family for a solid hour before my first break. So many people came through the line that I'm still in awe today just thinking about it. Tracie started out by my side with Andy just on the other side of her. They had one job—to take care of my every need. At the end of the first hour, the line subsided. I remember thinking when I saw the end of the line, "Oh my gosh, is that all that are coming?" But it's okay, God's in control. When the last person came through the receiving line is when I was informed that they had closed the doors so I could have a break. There were plenty more people that I had to greet that day.

After my break, we got the line started again, and we are back to it. This is when I started seeing the Hueytown Soccer Team trickle in. I remember the gratitude that ran across my heart. These fifteen- to eighteen-year-old boys were the ones tapped to carry my kids to their graves as pallbearers. I believe I got to thank each one of them before the service. There were breaks for my hedge. Tracie didn't like sitting down and leaving me, but they all needed to rotate and remain fresh. That was the only way I would make it through the day. Before I knew it, Kevin was beside me and handed me a bottle of water. Not long after he got there, a very humorous moment happened. I want you to understand that it wasn't all bad. There were little moments that I think God placed in my life to give me a breath. So what happened? Well, I was "hit on" at my kids' funeral. I remember looking at Kevin and I asked him, "Is what just happened what I think just happened?"

He just looked at me and responded, "Yes, brother, you just got hit on at your kids' funeral." I never saw that woman again, but I believe it was God. He needed to give me just a small smile so I could keep going. After that small humorous moment happened, my gauntlet continued.

Lunchtime came, and I was taken back to a dining area to eat. You would think that I would have a minute to just sit. But no. I felt as though I was an actor or something because there were people surrounding me, attending to my every need—things like getting the makeup off my collar from women hugging me, making sure I had food, and what my next steps were going to be. I will have to say that even though this was a terrible day, I could not have asked for better people to be around me. I got to spend a couple of minutes with my family members to assess how the day was going. That is when Erin's best friend from Mississippi was brought in.

Beanie had called me a couple of days before. As we talked, she asked me for something. On the last trip that she and Erin took together, my sister bought them a matching set of mood rings. Those mood rings had the kids' names on them, and that's what Beanie wanted. Of everything that we had, she wanted a $.99 mood ring with Erin's name on it. As soon as I got off the phone, I went straight to Erin's room and placed that mood ring on my pinky to give to Beanie when I saw her. When I took the ring off and gave it to her, it left a green-colored ring around my finger, which drove everyone nuts. But there was no time to deal with it because I was informed that two busloads of people had just arrived from Mississippi. They were keeping them outside until I finished lunch. So my gauntlet continued.

It was such a terrible day that I had yet another bright spot. All of Peyton's and Erin's friends and teammates from their former school in Mississippi were here. I think it was God again. The soccer teams from Tishomingo County High School were able to meet the soccer teams from Hueytown High School. It warmed my heart to see them all sitting in a section of the church talking and laughing with one another. There was just another pause. The next hour in the receiving line was a blur to me. I don't remember everyone that came through, but I do remember there were people that came and paid their respects from all parts of our lives.

The funeral service was nothing short of amazing. Three girls from the youth group at FBCPG sang a couple of songs. The previous youth minister came and said a few words and then sang a song himself. The new youth minister said a prayer that really got the ball rolling, but it was time for Brother Davin to make his appearance. Brother Davin started by reading the Beatitudes. If you remember, that was what was laid on me to read at Peyton's bedside the day of donation. It's Matthew Chapter 5. I had no idea where he was going next, but I believed God was leading him. He first started talking about the gauntlet and how you could drink it away, shoot a vein for it, or participate in other activities. That prelude brought him into the story of John the Baptist. He wound up paralleling the death of John the Baptist to the death of the kids. I was simply blown away. At the end of the sermon, he made a statement that I believe eased everyone's pain. He said if you knew the kids, then you knew they did everything together. Where you saw one, you saw the other. Wasn't it fitting that they died together as well?

As the service ended and they were being prepared for transport to the gravesite, I saw the first blip in the plan of events. I followed the kids out to the hearses. As they were loaded up, I realized there was no plan to get me to the cemetery. Here I was separated from my hedge for the first and only time that day. My brother-in-law threw me in a car and drove me to the cemetery. What I found out later was that Tracie left her purse where we ate, Kevin couldn't get the car into the funeral procession because of the crowd, and Radar and Jennifer went with their families. It was a mess, but it all worked out.

The cemetery wasn't but about five miles from the church. I don't know exactly how many cars came, but I'm willing to bet that the last car didn't pull out of the church until we had arrived at the cemetery. There were police escorts at every intersection. It was a true honor for my children. Peyton was carried to the gravesite first. It was a wonderful sight to see that the entire soccer team surrounded my babies as they were carried to the site. Every one of the boys looked awesome and was wearing his soccer jacket. Erin followed up secondly with the remainder of the team and coaches. They were given a few moments to pay their final respects before the service started.

You really don't get to see every side of the people who are in the kids' lives. That day, I saw a different side of Trey Cutrell's heart. He was Peyton's soccer coach at Hueytown and was tapped to speak at the graveside service. He told the stories of the kids during his coaching time with Hueytown. He shared a few inside stories that only he, the kids, and I knew about. He talked about Peyton's courage and how Peyton didn't like him very much at the beginning. He spoke of the game that changed Peyton's attitude toward him and the game of soccer as well. It took me back to the time that this actually happened. Peyton was knocked out right in front of the boys' bench during a game. Trey had gotten upset with him and was yelling at him as he was coming to and getting up. After the game was over, Coach Cutrell spoke with me. He apologized to me for the way he treated my son. I remember asking Trey if he loved my son and was just trying to better him. Trey responded by saying, "Yes." That's when I informed Trey that I didn't see him do anything wrong. He brought a lot of that story up that day at the graveside service. He then moved to Erin. Erin was my pistol. My righteous little teenage girl. She didn't have many boyfriends because, quite frankly, they were all scared of her. Trey spoke of the one and only time that he tried to coach Erin. She was running down the field one day during a game, and Trey tried to tell her to play wider on the field.

Erin stopped midstride and turned toward the bench where he was standing and yelled at the top of her lungs, "Don't start with me!" She did not realize it was the coach that had said it because he was standing with the boy's team. They were always goofing off and ribbing the girls. There would be times that they were trying to help, but the girls just took it as they were playing with them. The look on her face when she realized it was the coach was unmistakable. Coach Cutrell said that it carried him back and made him feel like a fourteen-year-old boy all over again. Even though Erin apologized a hundred times for it, that story stayed with her to the grave. Coach Cutrell lightened up a very hard time in my life, and I am grateful to him for this to this day. At the end of the service, as everything was being finalized, I saw a moment of realization of how this impacted other parents in the community. There was a father in the group who was clutching his daughters as he was sobbing at the gravesite. The expression on his face was unique. It took me a while to realize why. He was destroyed by this. His daughter played soccer with Erin. At the same time, as he was clutching his girls, he was grateful that it wasn't him burying his kids.

After the service, we left the cemetery and went to the church. After all, I'd only eaten twice today, so I had to eat again. The church put on a potluck dinner. It was very good. I still had an issue though. The news crews were still out front. They would not seem to leave. I couldn't go out and face them. It was not happening. There was no way that I could be on air. The church swept in and saved the day again. They handled media relations very well. There was a very good clip on the local news. After the meal, we went back to the cemetery. We looked over the flowers that were laid on the graves, and I remember talking about how beautiful the day was—how everything went so well when it could have gone so differently. We finished the day watching the sun set and went home because, you know, it was time to eat again. So there it is—seventeen and fifteen years of love, work, memories, hardships, and joys finished in a mound of dirt.

What Is a Champion?

You have heard the events of the darkest time in my life where my gauntlet has started. I want to paint a picture for a second to help you realize what this is like. Try to imagine that you are on a beach and the waves of the ocean are rolling in during a storm. Imagine as well a rock that is half buried in the sand. At first, the waves hit hard, but the rock stands. After a while, as each wave hits, the rock starts to move. Those waves hitting that rock are just like the hits that you have heard about during my first week. The rock stands strong at the beginning, but as the waves come, the rock relents.

I really didn't cry that much this week. It was terrible, but I had family and friends that kept me going. In some respects, time flew by. But in others, time seemed to stand still. The next couple of days really flew by. My birthday was the next day, and it seemed that I didn't really even remember it. I still had a lot to do, and quite frankly, I didn't even think about my birthday. What a way to celebrate forty-three years of life!

My grandmother's ninetieth birthday was another story entirely. Her birthday was on the 15th—just four days after I buried the kids.

She is elderly and had simple desires on her birthday. She wanted us all to go to Ryan's Steakhouse to eat. So here I was, at a restaurant with sports memorabilia all over the walls, in a place that the kids always loved to go eat. I remember it like it was yesterday. I did not break down or shed a tear. It didn't even phase me, that is, until I walked up to the bar and came across spaghetti. Then I fell apart. I completely lost it. Through all the serious stuff I had dealt with, I came apart over spaghetti? I never saw that one coming. I truly believe that God will control this for you if you let him. He guided me through that first week so masterfully. Then he let it hit me a little. Spaghetti, wow. I'll tell you, Peyton never found a bowl of spaghetti he didn't like. I have turned away from many plates, but not Peyton. No, sir. I believe you could have mixed dog food up with some noodles and put spaghetti sauce on it and Peyton would tell you how good it was for days. It was quite humorous. Erin would make fun of him time and time again. He would just smile and say that she just didn't understand how good it was. Why this memory? Or maybe better worded, this set of memories? The psychology world can explain it away, but until you live it, you will never understand. The sight of it, smell of it, and the taste of it will still put me in a tailspin of depression to this very day. It will consume my thoughts and my actions until I just let it run its course. Yeah, I know, easier said than done. There were so many of these days, and I'm going to talk about them, but this was the start of the rock relenting.

A few days later brought a day that was equally as tough, but one I had to get through just the same. It was the day that the high school soccer teams had to resume their season. I knew that I had to finish the season, but I didn't want to. The last thing on my mind was soccer. Hueytown High School was mourning as well, though. It was time to take on this part of my life. The booster club had talked to me and was planning to do a tribute to the kids. I had gotten the kids' jerseys framed and had decided to give one set to the school. Tonight would be a good time to give it to them. The news media has made several attempts at an interview. I have avoided that like the plague. Now it is something that I am going to deal with. I decided to contact Rick Burgess from a local radio show that is broadcast nationwide. He advised me on handling media relations at this time. I have decided to talk, but I just needed a little more time. He was a godsend. He probably doesn't even remember me, but I am grateful for the time he invested to get me through this time. I was never approached that night by the news, but they were there. The evening started off with being asked to speak to the boys' team. It didn't take but a second to decide what I was going to say. They needed my champion speech. I had given it a few years ago when I was coaching softball, and they needed to hear it. This motivational speech takes me back to when I was sixteen, and it's a true story. Well, with a little dramatic effect to get the point across.

What is a champion? If you are like I was when I was your age, it was the person or team with the most points at the end of the game. The winner, right? When I was sixteen, I was invited to an exposure camp at the University of Michigan for wrestling. It was an awesome experience and one that my parents had to have paid a fortune for. The second day there, they put together a tournament to see what we could do. Right off the bat, I drew a Junior National Champion. This kid was good. He didn't beat me badly, but I lost. I'm sixteen, so I didn't take it well at all. After all, this camp could have determined my future. There were coaches there from the surrounding universities. It was one of those matches where I could do nothing right and he could do nothing wrong. Every move he made, and every move I made, well, he countered. After the match was over, my frustration got the best of me. I spotted a garbage can and gave it a good kick as I went out the door. I was unaware that the coach from Duke University was following me out. He walked out right behind me and asked if I was okay. I apologized for losing my temper. I was embarrassed. This is when he talked to me and literally changed my life and how I think about competition. He asked me the same question, "What is a champion?" You guessed it; I told him that it was the winner.

He just gave me a smile and began to speak, "The wins and losses will come to us all in life. A champion has more to do with fight, courage, and the willingness to see it through to the end. If you can look into the eyes of your opponent, teammates, and coaches and know, without a doubt, that there was nothing more you could do—you have done everything that was possible to compete—then you are a champion. You prepared, fought, and shook hands after the competition. That is what a champion is."

I told this story to these kids and then looked at them. They were pumped up. That is when I put the extra "*mojo*" into the mix. Here I am—I am not quitting. I am not giving up. I am going to see this through. This is what the kids would have wanted, so here I am to cheer you on so you can finish it. Then we huddled in, and I prayed over the team. I believe that it touched everyone's hearts that night, including mine. The boys' team lost that night. Peyton was not at center mid or forward. (Those were the positions that he played through the season.) They not only lost their friend; they lost an important part of their team. This is what gave me an extra hurdle. I felt responsible. Peyton was mine. He was my responsibility. My loss was also a community's loss, and quite frankly, it took some time to get over this.

I want to go back to halftime for a second though. The booster club did a wonderful dedication to the kids. We had a balloon release. I dedicated the jerseys, which are now at the school in the trophy case beside a pro football player's jersey. What I didn't see coming was that the opposing team gave me a peace lily. The players in this sport are some great kids. I know that it is like every other sport and there is bad sportsmanship from time to time, but you have to be a special breed to play this sport. These two high school seniors and captains honored their team and the sport in an immeasurable way. I thank them for that.

Do you not know that in a race all runners run,
but only one gets the prize? Run in such a way
as to get the prize. Everyone who competes
in the games goes into strict training. They
do it to get a crown that will not last, but we
do it to get a crown that will last forever.

(I CORINTHIANS 9:24–25)

God's Woodshed

There are a few things that I left out during the first few weeks because they were instrumental in my walk. One is what I want to talk about now. I would like to tell you about how it came to pass about speaking on a national radio show.

We were doing thank-you cards, and God pressed on me to deliver two in person. The first card included a letter addressed to the former youth minister from Erin, which I will address later. The second thank-you card was to Brother Daven, the pastor who preached at the kids' funeral. I started toward Pelham and stopped at the Walmart for a restroom break. In the restroom, there was a man standing inside the door. It seemed a little odd to me until I turned around and saw what seemed to be his kid going between the stalls. Okay. It makes sense now. He is waiting on his boy. Another young child walked in and started reaching for the soap. He was probably around two or three years old. I reached over and pumped out some soap and put it in his hand. The boy went to the shorter sink, and that man helped him turn on the water. At that moment, God told me to bear witness to that man. It was nothing major—just tell him who I was and tell him to told his baby tight. Well, here comes my stubbornness. I'm crushed. I'm not the man for this. So I walked out. I ran into the man two other times in the store. I turned and ran. I've been through enough. "Come on, God. Cut me some slack." Then I promise this happened. The lights dimmed in the store and nearly went out. This huge wave of grief hit me. All I could think of was that God had dropped me. I started praying. "Lord, please don't drop me. I can't do this myself. I need you." The lights came on brighter than they usually were, and He told me to get on to Pelham.

I met Brother Daven in his office, and we spoke for about a half hour. That is when I let him know that I was not sure why I was there. "God told me to come so here I am." Brother Daven just smiled at me and said that he knew why. He told me about the church family there in Pelham that had prayed for me. Today was the day that they would get to put a face with the name. Then he asked me if I had eaten. I told him no and that I would go wherever he led. We then went to the youth building, and I met part of his Wednesday night congregation. After we ate, Bother Daven put a microphone in my hand. I probably spoke for about five minutes to about fifty people.

God got my attention that day and told me to start speaking. I had been talking to Rick Burgess privately, and he had been giving me advice on how to deal with the media. This day was when God laid it on my heart to speak out publicly.

I don't know why I'm being told to speak. I am so flawed. The devil has huge stones that could crush me. God made a promise to me though. If I am obedient to Him, He will make it perfect. He did with the funerals, and I have to trust Him now. Faith is an amazing thing. Glorifying God for what He has done for me is easy. I am the only thing standing in His way. He has given me peace and love through all of this beyond imagination. I'm not going to run anymore. I can't. It is too important to Him. If I see that man again at Walmart, we're going to talk. I don't care if tears and pain come from it.

As it is said in John—the punch line for Christians—you see it on Bible covers and purses, "For God so loved the world He gave His only begotten Son." I got a glimpse of that pain. We beat Jesus; we ridiculed him, tortured him, and then killed him. Now he is our pathway to heaven.

He said to them, "Go into all the world
and preach the Gospel to all creation."

(MARK 16:15)

Forgiveness

Rick and Bubba have a radio program that is nationally syndicated and is based in Birmingham. I have to say that they are a pretty good group of guys. If you remember earlier, I told you that I had made the decision to speak out to the media, but I needed time. Well it took me about three weeks to sort it out. I had contacted Rick earlier, and he helped me get through the first soccer game. He prepared me for what to say, even though it never came to fruition. That genuine courtesy is what made me use this show as a megaphone. After all, the kids' deaths were national news. My understanding was that it was printed in the New York Times Daily. I got donations from as far as Montana to help bury them. It was a big deal to the country, not just to me. I needed to respond, but until this point, I didn't know how. I spent a couple of mornings seeing the inner workings of the show and talking to Rick. You never really know what to expect from public personality figures. There are some characters out there, and well, they could be "a mixed bag of nuts" as Radar calls it.

There are two things that made me realize that I was in the right place. First, he never asked once to put me on air, nor did he once ask to quote me. He did ask to air one thing that we spoke about privately, but I will go into that later. The second was how he handled me. The first thing he said to me was that he was no different from me. He was just a few years ahead in his process. It's not a quote, but it was the gist of it. I felt better. After a few days of talking and dealing with my obstacles, I asked to go on air. It wasn't for five minutes of fame. I had to deal with the enormous responsibility I felt. Rick was gracious enough to give me a time slot on his show. I really hate that I did not meet Bubba. He was not at the show that day.

My time slot started with Rick introducing me. The looks of the other guests were unmistakable. If you are going through the same thing, then you know the look that I am speaking about. The look of almost being horrified. I started off by thanking Rick and the staff. Then I went straight into thanking people. I remember that I held it together pretty well until I got to the prayer warriors of the world. I had to mention them. Can you imagine the power of hundreds of thousands of people praying for you? Someone thought enough to ask God to comfort me without having a clue of who I am? I remember it well. "And to the prayer warriors of the world, you have no idea who God lays on your heart to pray for. Someone that you will probably never meet nor know what happens to them. For those who have prayed for me, I want you to know that I am grateful." Please take solace in knowing that your prayers did not go unheard. My faith is stronger than ever because of you.

There was another thing God laid on my heart to speak about, and that was on forgiveness. I had no idea if the other lady that was involved in the accident was listening to the radio. God laid it on my heart to include her in my forgiveness; I had to let her know. I told the world that from what I gathered, this was just an accident. Because this was an accident, there was nothing to forgive, but if it needed to be said, I forgave her.

As the slot was closing, Rick thanked me for coming. During the break he looked at me and asked if it was okay to share the cell phone conversation that we had in private. Do you know what God's blessing feels like? It is like a warm blanket that just wraps you. I just nodded my head in approval, and he started the next segment with it.

I had told him that I was worried about opening Peyton's and Erin's phones and going through them. I knew that I had good kids, but this was their interpersonal world I had never entered. I had never opened their phones. I had always wanted the kids to share things with me but also wanted them to have some privacy in their own world. Well, it worked. There was nothing really bad. Peyton had a few slang jokes and a video of them being pulled in a shopping cart behind another kid's vehicle, and Erin had about five-hundred pictures of the new pop band that she adored. They both were believers and warriors for God. They both had conversations with other kids that made each of them have to stand firm on God's Word. I was so proud. Anyway, Rick never went into this other than bringing it up and saying that we need to go through our kids' phones before they die, not after. I did not do him justice in that. He was masterful in the way that he spoke. It was another hard day, but one that needed to be done.

So I commend the enjoyment of life, because
there is nothing better for a person under
the sun than to eat and drink and be glad.

(ECCLESIASTES 8:15 NIV)

65

Pet Peeves

You deal with many things while facing the death of loved ones, but one of the most difficult things to deal with is people. When you are in hell like this, what can someone say to you? I have talked to many people that go through what I have been through to some measure, and this subject always comes up. I have noticed that pet peeves are different for individuals, but if you are a support person, this chapter is for you.

One lady, who had lost her husband and is a dear friend to me, said that her hot button was when someone would approach her and say either, "I know what you are going through," or "I can't imagine what you're going through." It makes you want to laugh and choke the life out of them at the same time.

She said it would make her think, *Do you think that my life is so bad that you can't even imagine it? You can't even imagine that it could be so terrible?* If you don't know what to say, then say nothing. This isn't really focused on the person. It has more to do with us redefining who we are. You know what I am talking about, right? What do you say to someone that you care about who is going through something like this? It is awkward. Trust me when I say this. It rang so loudly that I notice it, too. I think that awkwardness is one of the hardest things for a grieving person to go through. I don't think there is a right way to deal with it. I know that one of my bigger struggles at the beginning was the isolation from the people. I had a lot of close friends that walked through this with me, but the isolation from others—the not knowing what to say or do by others—would hurt. It took me some time to realize that they were not treating me differently because of me. It was because they didn't want to face the mortality of this for themselves. They could not relate, so they would avoid. Avoidance is hard, and people have a tendency to make things worse with no clue why.

However, my pet peeve comes when someone would tell me that I am not grieving yet. "You are in shock, and it will come." Really? Okay, let me explain something that is obvious to the grief world. First, death brings us to the same plane. There are differences, but if you have truly grieved, then you know what they are going through. If things are bad, telling them that it is going to get worse may not be the thing that you need to tell them. I heard this repeatedly over the first couple of months, and it was difficult to control my anger. I'm crying all the time, and my emotions are all over the place. How can I be in shock? If I am in shock, then how is telling me that I'm in shock beneficial? It drove me nuts. I remember that one person said that their pet peeve was when people that they didn't know would try to counsel them. They would give them their number and truly expect a call. I know that helping to fix things can be hardwired into a person, but there are things that you cannot fix. All you can do is make things worse. It is a fact. Please leave the counseling to the professionals. Every one of them that I have encountered realizes that grieving is a process for which they cannot change the timetable.

There are some beneficial things that you can say. If the person is a Christian, then there is power in prayer. Telling them that you are praying for them helps. It is usually a pet peeve if they are not a believer, but praying could change their lives anyway. I truly believe that all of the people praying for me helped with my situation. There is power there. It doesn't have to be a long drawn-out prayer, but just lifting them, if only for a minute, does wonders for them. I believe it.

The grievers have to turn to God themselves, but you can help. The other is just listening. A lot of things that still go through my mind is irrational. It really doesn't matter what is said. Conversation is a good thing. It could be that you give them the latest in sports. They would not be listening, but it will get their mind to working, and that is what is important.

And let us consider how we may spur one
another on toward love and good deeds.

(HEBREWS 10:24 NIV)

A Box of Love

I 've made many mistakes in my life. The ones that hit hardest you don't realize until they are over. I was given a box to hold mementos of the kids. We had issues at the beginning with finding a stuffed animal that Erin had kept since she was four years old. She named it "Kitty" and carried it everywhere with her. I wanted to bury it with her. It just seemed right. My sister looked and looked for Kitty during that week and came up empty. So many people were worried that I would come apart over that, but it was just another place that God covered me with love. But the problem remained. Kitty was missing, and that had to be dealt with. So here I go. I got Peyton's wallet and put it in the box, and now it is time to dig in Erin's room to try to find Kitty. It didn't take me long to find it, but what I found with that little stuffed animal was something that I had no idea would tear me apart as it did. As I mentioned earlier, there was a letter written to the youth pastor at the kids' church who had resigned for family issues. I remember back to the conversation that the kids and I had when this happened. They were so upset that he left and they did not get a chance to say goodbye. My response to them was that maybe they needed to write him a letter. I will figure out how to get it to him when the time is right. Erin wrote that letter, but never got it to him. That letter warms my heart and tears me to shreds at the same time. I am not going to talk about the letter in its entirety because it was addressed to him. There is one place that I must bring up that has to do with her walk. She told him that she didn't go to church much and when she did, it wasn't that great. He was the only one that spoke to her outside the church. This and telling him that he was the reason she rededicated her life to Christ are the germane parts to my pain and mistakes.

You never know how your walk or your fall will affect others. I had some difficult times over the last four or five years, and I didn't lean on God. It's okay. That is my issue with God, right? Well, I have been shown by that letter that I was very wrong. My failure hurt my daughter's walk. What would have happened if she would have died and not gotten back into church? Where would my kids be spending eternity? Talking about a blow to the heart. There are so many lost kids out there who don't know God. I am grateful to this youth minister. I was trying to find my way and lost sight of helping them find theirs. Sometimes that's how you find it—by showing others. Please don't let this fall on deaf ears. Make sure the people around you are able to find their way. Don't be their stumbling block.

Peyton had a hundred-dollar bill that he carried in his wallet. There are some lessons that you cannot teach your kids. That is why it takes a village to raise a child. This is the story that Radar shared on Facebook. Thank you, Radar. I am truly grateful for your influence in my kids' lives.

Crusty
A Lesson on Self-Discipline

On April 19, 2014, a number of us went to The University of Alabama's A-Day game. After the game, we decided to go to Habenero's Mexican Grill. When we finished our meal, Chris and Peyton Spain joined me in the parking lot. Peyton began to tell me that he had been doing some landscaping work and earning some extra money. I asked, "What are you going to spend it on?"

He said, "I don't know. I have a $100 bill left. Maybe a video game or something."

The stage was set for a lesson. I began to tell him, "When I was a little older than you are now, I had a reputation of being very tight with spending money. It was often joked about among friends. They would say, 'Oh, Radar, come off of some of those crusties in your wallet,' or 'You need to get some of those crusties from your sock drawer and just buy you one.' At this point, Chris began to share a few stories from the past about this with Peyton.

I explained to Peyton, "What my friends didn't know is oftentimes those crusties were set back with an intended purpose. There would be a goal or an accomplishment attached to them. When it was accomplished, it was then okay to spend it. Just a few months ago, there was a $500 bonus opportunity at work. It was going to be very challenging to meet the numerous goals that were outlined to earn it. I decided to pursue it, and upon earning the bonus, I would set aside about $130 for a rod and reel combo. The bonus was earned, and it was purchased. I enjoy fishing as a hobby, but never before spent that much on a rod and reel. I guess that I never took it that seriously to buy higher-quality gear." Peyton decided that day that he was going to hold on to that $100 bill. Chris quickly dubbed it "crusty" and was very excited to do so. I explained, "It is okay to spend crusty, but only after you have earned it. When you do, always set a goal to replace it as soon as possible and set a new goal."

On April 8, 2015, we were at UAB Hospital after Peyton had passed away. Chris received a call from his sister Sandy. She let him know that crusty had been found in Peyton's room. It's difficult to convey the look in his eyes as he shared this information with me. There was an overwhelming pain of sudden loss for both of his children, Peyton and Erin. At the same time, they were filled with the pride of a father with yet another example of how they made him proud of them. It moved me to realize that the small discussion we had left such an impression on him. Almost a year had passed since we had that conversation. The measure of discipline displayed for a sixteen- to seventeen-year-old young man to not spend that $100 bill is a testament to the importance of the goal he set with it.

Chris feels as though it was the original $100 bill. Maybe it was a long-term goal, or it was a second or third crusty. Either way, it is framed with Peyton's soccer jersey in honor of his goal setting and self-discipline.

Thank you, Peyton Spain. I am honored by your example, and I am hopeful that by sharing your story, you will be honored as well.

Radar

This letter helps remind me of what it takes to raise a child and that a teaching moment can come from anywhere at any time. I stare at that jersey that is framed often. I have not hung either of them on the wall yet. It just doesn't seem right. It will come though. I just have to decide where I want to put them.

These types of things build up. I have two soccer balls in framed cases on my desk. They were both from the same soccer camp at UAB. It was a one-day clinic, and the kids got to watch a college soccer game afterward. The camp was fun for them, but the soccer balls were the focus. I was broke. I had always gotten them a ball every year, but could not afford it this time. These free balls got them through the fall league. Erin's ball actually was a game ball twice during the season. The memories that that ball has accumulated are amazing. Peyton's is autographed by the boys' team. I had thought about getting the girls to do the same. I decided against it—not so Peyton's would look different, but because Erin's ball is on the girls' team. It was the game ball twice and was at every practice that fall. I know it probably sounds a little dumb, but I don't want to cover up a dirt scuff from Tori or the sweat residue from Savannah catching it and saving a goal. You get the idea.

The soccer banquet didn't happen at the end of the season like in previous years. I think that the kids' hearts were just not in it. They finished the season. They fought the good fight, but it just took their hearts when my two couldn't finish it with them. They had a small get-together after the season and gave out awards. This is when I received Peyton's and Erin's sports letters. It was their first actual letter even though they have earned letters on their teams for a while. Kids just do not do letterman's jackets anymore, so I think it is one of the things that fell by the wayside. Peyton made the all-metro team as a sophomore as well. The last thing given out to the team was something that touched my heart. Birmingham United Soccer Association (BUSA) gave the entire team shirts. It was not a cheap T-shirt either. They were jerseys. The front of them said, "Donate Life," to represent the AL Organ Center and Peyton, and the back said, "SPAIN," with 10/5 underneath it, memorializing their numbers. Thank you, BUSA. It means a lot to me whenever I see those shirts being worn around town. I wear that shirt often, and the Hueytown letters are in my box as well.

I know that I have talked about athletics a lot and haven't really gone into the other aspects of their lives. But at the end of their school year, I had to finish it out. They were both pretty good students. Academically, they kept their grades up. A straggling C here or there kept them off the honor roll, but with the hand life dealt us, I was still very proud. Erin was so excited that she was going to go into theater the next year, where Peyton was and I had been. Peyton didn't like being in public much, so he spent most of his time building the sets and props. Erin was a chip off the old block. She would have loved what would have come in her life in high school. The kids talked about it often. The end-of-the-year awards involved him, though. He was inducted into the International Thespian Society. The night of the banquet was a double-edged sword, just like the others. It was a night of life and laughter. His friends were there, and it was a night to remember. When the signing part of the night came, I signed my son's name on the charter just as I had done roughly twenty-five years before when I signed mine. I received his cords for graduation as well. I remember laughing about the fact that his was purple and gold, while I had to wear a pink one on my graduation walk. This night sent me back into a depression tailspin. It was another reminder that their lives were cut short. They were snuffed out in the prime of life, when it was truly starting. His chords are in my box as well.

Teaching Erin how to drive was a difficult thing to do. She was headstrong and wanted to do it herself. I wound up having to teach her in a parking lot. I think it was more for my nerves than hers. The day that we spent in a church parking lot was comical. She would drive around in a big circle and smile. She was driving all by herself. She had to learn to park and back up unassisted. Peyton would not get in the truck with her, and I just couldn't. We found that the best way was to give her instructions and just let her figure it out. God was with us that day. I know it in my heart. We both lived through it, and nothing was destroyed, especially our relationship. She died three weeks before her sixteenth birthday, so she never actually got her license, but she had completed the driving exam at the school, so she was just clicking off the days. Her permit is in the box as well, and it really hurts to know that in three weeks she would have replaced it with a license.

Today that memento box is sitting on my dresser. A copy of Erin's letter to the youth minister along with Peyton's wallet, Kitty, and a few more mementos that I spoke about are placed there. Each of these things reminds me of so many different things. But they all roll up into one thing. That is love. Love enough to sacrifice; love enough to teach and place your children before you. Love enough to let go and let them live even though I am living the worst fear and consequence of letting go. One thing that I am not harboring is regret though. There are so many things that I wished I could have done differently, but I never left them. I stayed true to my commitment to raise them and loved them with all my heart. They knew it, and so did I.

Blessed be those who mourn, for
they will be comforted.

(MATTHEW 5:4 NIV)

Time for Help

The summer of 2015 was the hardest in the aftermath. I was not doing well and had started attending counseling. The Amelia Center was affiliated with UAB and the Alabama Organ Center. I had received a booklet about them. They specialized in grief. The center is for dealing with death, plain and simple—death of parents or death of children. Surviving death is their focus. They are based on donations, so it wasn't going to cost me anything to go. I thought about it for a few days before I went. After all, nothing is free, so what kind of service is a place like this going to give? It will be a token. But that is okay. I just need to satisfy friends and family, so it sounds like a plan. I made the call. The director took me himself. I figure it had to do with how public the kids' deaths were, but it could have been that it was just his draw in the case load. I really never talked about that with him. Robert, here is your chapter. I didn't have high expectations when I went, but I was going to take it seriously. I have a limited background in this field, so I knew what was coming. A whole lot of busy work and forms, right? WRONG! I really underestimated this group. They are as professional as they come and dedicated to what they do. What shocked me right off the bat and put things in perspective was when Robert said that he really couldn't help me yet. So many people walk into a place looking for that magic bean that can fix their lives. It doesn't exist. This is a process. I know you are probably thinking that you would have turned around and walked out after that statement, but I believe he is just that good at sensing and understanding the individual that he is working with. He did ask me a few questions before he made that statement. He was given an accurate picture of my support system and my mental status. I believe that he was able to drop the mask and be blunt. He didn't have that pill. He knew it didn't exist. He knew that I had friends and family that were dealing with my daily depression and emotional toil. He sat there patiently as I cried many times. There were a few sessions where I think the only words he said were "How is Chris?" at the beginning and "Time's up" at the end. I'm not going to bore you with the tears and turmoil of those sessions. Instead, I want to talk about some of the other ones.

I remember one session. I told you that I had some knowledge in this field, right? Robert said I knew enough to be dangerous. I believe he is accurate. I knew that he would get into me before it was over, but I really didn't see him get blunt and tell me the mistakes I was making—well, except for work. I'll talk about that later. First though, I came in having a real pity party. Poor pitiful me. After all, life sucked. I am fighting depression daily. I'm fighting to get up at lunch. I stayed in bed a couple of times, pretty much all day. So lunchtime was a big enough goal. He opened up a little more to me about his job. He never intruded on patient confidentiality. He didn't have to. He just told me that he dealt with a family that lost both of their kids, at different times. Well, I tell you. That put an end to my self-loathing. Can you imagine losing a child? Having to bring your other child through the grieving process only to lose that child, too? Wow, that was an eye opener. Hearing someone else's pain helped me in my own. A lot of times, it's just really easy to see the superficial side of life. You're bumping along in your own life, and you just don't notice the depths of other people's grief. This was one of my moments of stopping and smelling the roses—another spot in life that I got to see that others are going through similar things. I know I've said it a couple of times, but it's true. Knowing that you're not alone in what you're going through helps. There is strength in numbers. The word "club" came across my mind during this time. It is a term that I do not like hearing and do not wish to be a part of, but there's no way around it. When you go through this, you are dubbed into a club as it's called the club of parents who have lost their kids. It is a club that you never want to be a part of, but it's much larger than you realize.

I have had multiple sessions with Robert, and I told you that there was really one time that he got into me. I know why, and he is right. Throughout this year, I struggled with routine. I would go to work for a little while and then lay out for a little while. I just could not get myself together. It hits a much deeper topic. A topic I still struggle with today. What do you do when you lose your purpose? I worked to give us the needs for our family to help us survive. That's gone. My purpose was over. This is the bear that Robert had to fight and is the 800-pound gorilla that I am still fighting today. When you have such a big problem to deal with, the best way to deal with it is by taking it one step at a time. Start with the small stuff. Next thing you know, you will be on your way to solving the problem. This problem is no different. It's just more complex. What Robert helped show me was that my purpose in life is a long-term transition. It is not something that will be fixed in a day, in a year, or in twenty years. It will continue to evolve for the rest of my life. If you are a grandparent, you'll know what I'm talking about. Your kids have their own families, their own homes, and their own lives. Your purpose in raising them and financially supporting their every need has evolved. The problem that I've come upon is that my kids' deaths finalized this process without transition. I will never be a grandparent. I don't get to see Peyton and Erin stand on their own two feet in their own lives. My role as a father has been brought to a fiery end. The point I'm trying to bring to light is that your children start cutting their own teeth and start making their own lives without your need for support. It is usually a slow transition and evolves into years.

Robert stayed on me about getting back to work and never letting up. He knew that going back to work would help in establishing a routine. I think now, looking back, that it is a key to your process. Don't get me wrong, I dealt with a lot of my issues more quickly because I wasn't in a routine like most. I don't know where I am in my first year of grief, but I seem to be ahead of them.

Thinking back, I really believe Robert had my number. In the summer of 2015, Father's Day was coming up. I was struggling. I didn't want to deal with it. Heck, I didn't know how to deal with it. I remember looking at Robert and telling him that I just wanted to run and go to Keokuk, Iowa. No one would know me there. I would not get a "Happy Father's Day" from anyone. A phrase that I knew would stab me in the heart. So I told him I wanted to run. I did not want to face it nor deal with it. He just smiled at me, and he told me it would be okay. I could run, and we would deal with it next year. There's no shame in it. After all, you're dealing with a lot. Now, I don't know if he knew that would slap me in the face or not. He might have just been honest. But it struck a nerve in me. As another friend told me, I have never run from anything in my life. My friends, family, and counselor all said that I deserved a pass. Boy, that made me think for a little bit. I am not the type that runs. My personality commands that I hit things head on. I'm not going to sit around the house and read Facebook happy Father's Day wishes all day. I'm not going to lie in bed counting the minutes until it passes. So what do I do? I'll tell you what I did. If I've got to face it sooner or later, let's get it out of the way. So how did I deal with it? I decided to go back to where it all started. My first honeymoon was there, and it was a place that I took the kids every summer when they were young. It was the beach. I told you about my support system earlier. You know, the one Robert made sure I had in place. I'm still in the pits of hell in my life, so there are very few places that I'm actually going alone. Going out of town? My hedge was not going to allow that. Tracie was tapped to go. If you think this weekend was going to be candy and nuts and have a Merry Christmas, you're wrong. She was warned before we ever embarked. My goal was not to go enjoy the beach. My goal was to face Father's Day. Tracie was transformed into Erin that weekend. She was made to do all the things that Erin loved. I will have to admit that I did get a sadistic pleasure in making her pick up a starfish and a horseshoe crab at the Gulfarium. The weekend was spent collecting seashells during the day and chasing sand crabs at night. That's what the kids loved. So that's what we did. I don't know how Robert saw that coming, but when I described this weekend to him, I think he got a real understanding of my personality that day. I really think that is when he started changing his tone with me. He would get a lot firmer when my routine was involved. I don't know, but it could have just been part of his personality and the involvement of the depths of our relationship. Either way, shortly after this, Robert would get on to me when there was something I needed to do.

Thinking back, Robert never said a cross word to me except about work. The routine of work would help get me back on track. He didn't fight it at the beginning because I had other routines. I was going to the cemetery daily, taking care of the graves. The cemetery planted grass and did what they were supposed to do, but it was just not to my standard. So I took it to another level. I replanted grass and a dogwood tree. The grass that I planted was a high-end zoysia grass. I pretty much had a golf course putting green on their graves by the end of the summer. Robert helped me understand that this routine was important. I called them missions, but Robert understood it to be that I was caring for them still after their deaths. You can't just stop parenting and caring for your children, not when you are their entire support system. You have to have a transition. There has to be time. Robert understood this and helped me understand this. A lot of people were worried about me because I was at the cemetery every day, rain or shine. I would not miss a day. There were a lot of times that I would go twice a day, especially at the beginning. There were things that were coming into play. Headstones were being made; the bench was ordered, engraved, and brought in. This stuff had to be right. My kids were important enough, so I made sure of it. There was nothing more important. Let's face it; I didn't know how to function, so this is what I put myself into. This routine lasted most of the summer.

When fall came around, things started changing. That was when Robert started getting on to me. I was slowing down; the cemetery was done; depression was setting in. He pushed me to go back to work, and I tried. The part of me that hits things head on also is the part of me that recognizes when I screw up. When I went back to work, I couldn't do anything right. I broke, tore up, or did wrong everything I touched. I didn't know what to do, so I left work. I just told my boss that I thought I was ready, but I wasn't. Man did that upset Robert. The battles with work still somewhat continue. I now go to work every day that I'm supposed to, but I really struggle getting there on time. I have not seen Robert in a couple of months, but it has primarily to do with this book. God has laid it on my heart to concentrate primarily on this. So now this book and work are the main two things in my life.

There were other things that we discussed. Can you believe that I was "hit on" during the funeral? I was also hit on at church a week later at the altar. The first time I was hit on, I was in the receiving line. I'm not myself, so I looked at Kevin, who was standing beside me, and asked him if that was what I thought it was. Kevin had a giggle in his voice and said, "Yeah, brother, you just got hit on at your kids' funeral." Robert and I spent most of the session on this. I believe it has to do with empathy for a tremendous loss. Either way in our session, Robert let me know that there are such things as funeral groupies. I truly believe that conversations start off genuine. I just think that people start putting their own agenda into what's going on. It is really easy to take advantage of someone when their mind is in another hemisphere. For me, loneliness can be destructive. I miss my kids. I've lost my routine. Heck, I've lost everything. I would spend hours playing video games on my phone, escaping from reality. Basically, Robert was very understanding and told me I just needed to stay the course. "Don't make decisions at this time in my life. Try not to destroy my relationships and keep from cultivating new relationships whenever possible." After all, you don't know others' intentions, and you cannot think rationally.

Robert knew Christmas was going to be tough. We had talked about it and knew it was going to be one of my biggest milestones. After all, Christmas day in 1997 was when Peyton was born. I would be dealing with Peyton's birthday on top of this major holiday. I took it on the same way I did Father's Day, except I decided to go to a place I had never been to. I got suggestions from my supervisor, from Robert, and from Radar on the sites of things to do in New Orleans. I faced Christmas morning and went to the cemetery. I then went by and ate dinner with Tracie's family. I packed Tracie up and brought her with me. We stopped at the beach and spent the night and then went to New Orleans where we spent three days. I guess we had a good time. We enjoyed the sites and did a lot of people watching. If you want to see unusual people, New Orleans is the place to be. I have to admit that this strategy did not work as well as I thought it would. Maybe it did. I don't know. I do know that it sent my mental status back six months. If I had not hit it head on as I did, maybe it would have put me back to the beginning. That would be just something that I would guess about. Either way, the next three months were difficult. It was the summer of 2015 all over again.

A counselor's job has to be difficult. You want to just grab hold and pull someone out of their despair, but you can't. You just got to sit there and watch that train wreck happen. All you can do is try to help them guide themselves out of the wilderness. I do not envy Robert's job. In fact, I have a great deal of respect for it. Thank you, Robert, for everything you've done.

Where there is no guidance, a people falls, but
in an abundance of counselors there is safety.

(PROVERBS 11:14 ESV)

It's Just Stuff

Dealing with the kids' deaths is hard enough, but there are aspects of the aftermath that make it even worse. Every day, something reminds you of them—whether it's a picture, a soccer ball, or some other little item. There comes a time when you have to deal with their stuff. Talking to other parents, I learned that this is one of the biggest monsters that you have to deal with. Cleaning out their rooms has got to be done. Some people don't do it at all. They'll leave a room intact for twenty years. It's just going to sit there and wait on you though. It will sit there until you have no choice but to make time for it.

My nephew had come back from college. To make a long story short, he needed his room back. It's not that I didn't want to deal with it; it was just that everything else had come in front of it. Now Peyton's room is on the front burner, and it's got to be cleaned out. I didn't know how to prepare myself for this. I didn't have a clue. The only thing I could do was tackle it as I have tackled everything else in my life—head on. I had gone into his room here and there and moved stuff around—maybe take something out or place something in there—but this was completely different. Tracie had offered to

89

help several times over when it comes to things like this. But what do you do? This is as personal as it gets. I'm going to get rid of my son's personal belongings. Don't get me wrong. There are some things I'm going to keep myself, but there was way more than what I needed. There is still some stuff in storage that I have not tackled yet, but this was the stuff in their daily lives. I decided to take Tracie up on her offer. It's been about four months since their deaths, and it was just time.

We had a pretty good plan. Tracie would go through the room, and I would sit on Peyton's bed and tell her what to do with it. I'm dealing with it, but not really. It is more she's dealing with it, and I'm sitting there watching. We started with his chest of drawers. She started pulling out clothes left and right. I have a lot of kids that have requested some of his clothes, and I figured that was the best place for them to go. After all, I couldn't wear them. He was about my size in high school, so unless I'm willing to drop about eighty pounds, it's not going to happen. It didn't take long for Tracie's "organizational" skills to come into play. We made a pile for this person and another one across the bed for another person. Before you knew it, there were stacks of clothes all over the room going to different destinations. Don't tell Tracie this, but she was a gem that day. She remained very patient with me even when I would get angry. I took the attitude at the beginning that this is just stuff. This isn't the kids. This is just a shirt or a pair of pants. You can get one just like it at the store, so it's no big deal. I tried to depersonalize it as much as I could. I think it helped, but that house of cards crashed on me several times.

There were so many of the items that I couldn't turn loose. For instance, socks. I needed socks, and that was one item that Peyton wanted name brands for. He loved his American Eagle socks. So I took them. Every time I wear them, I get the memory of Peyton and Erin telling me that I need to get more updated socks. My tube socks were so out of style. Tracie would talk about it, but I'd just ignore her. I think that's when she recruited the kids, and it was on. I don't care about style. They're socks, for goodness' sake. You won't see them. They're under your pants and inside your shoes. But somehow, the powers that be believe that I should still be in fashion even when I'm in the bathroom by myself with nothing on but shorts and socks.

It wasn't just clothes that we found in that chest of drawers. Even though my son was a mature seventeen-year-old, he was still a kid. I happened to run across a progress report from school with a D on it. Oh, he wasn't going to show me that. It was like a sixty-eight or a sixty-nine. But still it was a D. So just like every other kid in this world, he hid it in his sock drawer. That one made me cry. It wasn't from being upset or him trying to hide something from me. It was just another paper cut and feeling the hurt of my son being gone. I can't talk to him about it. I can't ground him. I can't give him another one of those speeches about "Son, this D is in English. If you can't bring it up to a C, you can't play soccer." All I could do was stare at that paper and miss my boy. I believe it took us about an hour to completely clean out that chest of drawers; then we moved on to his dresser.

His dresser was a little bit more difficult because it wasn't just clothes. Don't get me wrong, there were a lot of clothes to go through, but scattered throughout were souvenirs and trinkets of different kinds that he had accumulated over time. The biggest thing to deal with on his dresser was the XBox. I had just bought him a new XBox 360 for Christmas. The box was still sitting beside the dresser. When I unplugged it, I sort of felt as though I was unplugging him. I was unplugging us.

When he was young, we would play games. We would play football out in the yard or baseball, but as he became a teenager, he turned to the world of gaming. I had a choice. I can learn how to play Halo, or our relationship would distance. Through the years, we would play different games, but our favorite had to be Call of Duty. He had every one of them, and we would spend hours shooting each other and shooting anything that moved. He was much better at it than me. It was so embarrassing that I would catch myself going into his room and practicing when he was away. I thought I could be slick about it until one day he came back from vacation and asked me if I had been playing his game. I knew I had put all of the controllers back up exactly the way they were left. There was no way he would know. Have you ever heard of online gaming? I never knew those kids could actually send each other messages and have conversations. One of his online buddies asked him if there was something wrong. He had never played this badly before. Busted! What can I say? No way to hide it now. So from that day forward, I would let his online buddies know that it was his dad playing. The kids would usually say, "Hey, Mr. Spain, just stay in the back and don't get us killed." Virtual slaps hurt just as badly as the real thing. I read some of those messages between them when I was responding. It warmed my heart when I saw a conversation about how cool it was that Peyton's dad would sit down and play with him. Their dads wouldn't do it. I was terrible—they didn't hold back in telling me that—but Peyton didn't care. He would call me to play with him every weekend. Don't get me wrong, Erin loved getting in the mix, too. I didn't want to mention this because it's even worse to get your tail kicked by a teenage girl. Yep, she was good too—not quite as good as Peyton—but could give him a run for his money. His XBox is sitting in my room. I'm not going to get rid of it, but it's one of two things that I have not tackled yet. I will play it before long—probably after this book is done.

We finished the dresser and moved on to the nightstand. In the nightstand top drawer was the rest of his XBox accessories. That is why I moved to it next. That way, I could keep all of his XBox stuff together. It was full of sunglasses, arm bands from the trampoline place he loved, hacky sacks, and other stuff like that. The bottom drawer had his stuff he wore to the lake. My dad owns a place on Smith Lake and has since I was ten years old. I was raised on that lake and raised both of them there. When I was a single dad, between my first and second marriages, I couldn't afford a vacation. The best I could do was the lake. They loved it. We would have so much fun wake boarding, knee boarding, and especially tubing. They have caught so many bream from the end of the pier that I couldn't begin to tell you how many. As the kids got older, they got more independent. They got their own boating licenses and would take off on the Jet Skis themselves. I bet they knew every inch of that lake. It would cost Pops a fortune in gas. But it was a true love. This was the second thing that I have not been able to face yet. I figure it will come.

After all, I tackled the beach and survived it. It's just that we spent so much more time at the lake. It wasn't just a vacation place. It was our second home. Now it's three o'clock in the morning, and we are both exhausted. This couple-hour project has turned into a weekend thing.

The next day, we started tackling his closet. Kids are funny. One of the first things we ran across was one of his thick winter jackets. It still had the tag on it, and he swore to me that it was not there. He spent a couple of winters wearing a jogging suit jacket simply because he didn't like that jacket for whatever reason. If he had been alive when I found it, it would have made me angry. But all I could do was hug it because it was another thing that tied him to a specific memory. He never even wore it. Sometimes you just don't realize the generation gaps. I looked at that jacket and thought it has good pockets in it, it is thick, and it will be warm on a cold night. He probably looked at it and thought he would look like a nerd in it. That's why I gave it to Tracie to put on her boys. (My sadistic side is coming out again.)

It wasn't long until I came upon his ski bib. He had lost it and had to borrow someone else's bib on his last ski trip with the church. Yep, he is a guy, just like me. He lost it because he put it where it was supposed to be. He loved skiing. He would tell me all of the time that we needed to go. I would tell him that I never lost anything on the ski slope, so he shouldn't get his hopes up. Now I want to go just because he wanted me to. I would probably break something, but it would be worth it. I donated both of their ski outfits to the church. I am sure that there will be a kid that wants to go, but cannot afford to do it. Hopefully, this will be a game changer for them.

His shoes were the last thing that I went through. There were a couple of pairs that I could wear, but for the most part, he had bigger feet than me. I really hate that I gave a brand-new pair of Nikes to the clothes closet at church. I also have to admit that I looked a little funny with a teenager-style pair of shoes. This instance made me realize why so many men wear these bright shoes. They are wearing their kids' hand-me-downs. Peyton's feet didn't outgrow mine until right before his death, so this escaped me until I cleaned out his closet. We finished his closet and went to eat lunch that day. We were not done, even though his room was done. My agenda consisted of the kids' bathroom and the belongings from the car as well.

We decided to tackle the personal belongings from the car. My hedge dealt with cleaning out the car because I just couldn't. The people from the wrecker company didn't want me to even see it. I was told that the car was almost cut in half. There was blood throughout the car from the kids. It was a sight that I didn't need to see, so they took care of it, along with my dad. They brought everything back and placed it in a tub. It was left in the garage until I was able to go through it. Today was the day. There wasn't much stuff in there, but it was going to be difficult. It had the clothes that the kids wore to school that day, along with the soccer gear that they had just taken off before they got in the car. It was not what I expected, and I had a breakdown moment. I pulled Peyton's cleats out of the tub, and they stunk. He wasn't known for sweet fragrances when he sweated. But this was worse. The smell of dried blood where it was splattered on the cleats made it worse. I freaked out inside. That was my baby's blood splattered on the cleats. It was a moment of realization again. This dance between shock and realization goes on constantly. It does not just happen at the beginning. In fact, I still go through it today. I washed what I could, but everything from that tub pretty much had to be destroyed.

The only thing left was the bathroom. I really thought it would be the easiest thing to deal with out of this day. I was terribly wrong. There was some of the stuff that I could push into Erin's room to deal with later, such as her makeup. There was so much more that was dealt with that tore me apart. One of the senses that you have is called the olfactory sense. It is basically the sense of smell and how it triggers a memory in your brain. It is more complex than that, but this simplistic definition gives you the idea. The bathroom is the home of what you smell like. I didn't realize how so until we started this final leg of the journey. Peyton's body wash hit first, but I rolled with it. Erin's shampoo and conditioner were the first knockdown blow. I don't know if the day just built up or if this was the monster I had made it out to be all by itself. Tracie had to really push me through this part because I would go down every time I would get into their vitamins or their deodorant. I kept their toothbrushes as well as a pair of Peyton's contact lenses. I kept Erin's hairdryer but pretty much got rid of everything else. All of the stuff from this weekend was difficult to deal with. If I knew I wanted to keep it or was not sure, it went into a big plastic tub that is still sitting on my bedroom floor. But I finished the day. I got everything that I needed out of the rooms where my nephew would move. I think that this day got the best of Tracie, too. When we finished, we both just lay on Peyton's bed and cried.

This beat me down to the point that I didn't tackle Erin's room for two more months. It was well into the fall of the year when I got the courage to knock this out. Before I left work for the weekend, I let my supervisor know what I was doing to warn him that I may not be back on Monday. God laid it on his heart to tell me to keep their mother in mind when going through their things. Tracie did a wonderful job helping Peyton's room, so I asked her if she could handle doing it again. She gladly accepted, and we tackled Erin's room. We pretty much went through the same process. I sat on the bed while Tracie did everything. She was a real trooper. Erin didn't have much stuff in her room either. The things that she did have were hard for us to get rid of. I know I portrayed Erin to be 10-foot tall and bullet-proof, but the fact is that she was very petite. Sandy had done most of her clothes shopping with her as she got older. There are just some things that a dad can't do. So Aunt Sandy came in and took her shopping. I didn't even know they made jeans in a size 00. Where do you get these things? I know that there are junior miss departments and stuff like that, but really? 00? Wow. Anyway, back to the task at hand. She was so petite that there wasn't going to be any way that we were going to find friends who could wear this stuff. Don't get me wrong, I'm sure there are plenty of girls out there that are as small as my Erin was; it's just that at this time, it blew my mind.

Girls are so much different than boys. It seemed like everything she owned either sparkled in some way or had a girly smell to it. We tackled her dresser first. She had three drawers of unmentionables. Unfortunately, we had to put all of that in the garbage. Even if we did give it away, I don't think I would want someone else to wear those articles. Then we got into the two drawers of jeans and shorts that I spoke about. We then quickly moved into her T-shirts. These were something that we could deal with. Most of her shirts were smalls, with a few mediums sprinkled in she probably stole from Peyton. I also found a shirt or two that were mine. I remember thinking that it must have looked as if she was wearing a tent if she put on my shirt. It's a weird thing about women. Somehow wearing their brother's or their father's clothes makes them feel closer to us. I'm a guy, so I don't understand, but I know there's something there. Thinking back on it now, they were all in her sleep shirt drawer. It just made me smile when I found them. It helped me to realize my baby girl loved me as much as I loved her.

When we got through with the clothes in her dresser, we decided to switch gears. We tackled the drawer full of nail polish as well as the things that were on top of her dresser. It was primarily makeup. It was very difficult to pick up an eyeliner pen without realizing that this is what she put on every morning before school. It was the same with all of her makeup. I didn't want to get rid of any of it, but what was I going to use it for? Am I just going to sit it in a bin for me to have to deal with again? No. I have to let it go. I threw a lot of that away. There was plenty more makeup though. I ran into her travel box next. It was a cute little makeup box that had her name on it. It was full of makeup that she was currently using—a lot of which was still brand new. Whom do I give this to? I thought about Radar's daughter. The problem with giving it to her is that she doesn't wear much makeup and she has a darker complexion (I've been told that that's important). I told Tracie to ask her daughter if she would like it. This was one of the best decisions I have made yet. Her daughter uses that makeup box all the time. I see her carry it out with her clothes every time she goes somewhere. What I thought would pierce my heart gives me a tremendous smile.

We moved through the dresser and got to her chest of drawers. They were basically empty. Erin hung up most of her clothes in her closet, so it didn't take us long to clear the chest of drawers out. On top of that chest of drawers was a Dr. Pepper bottle. I remember when she got it and drank the Dr. Pepper. It was a retro-looking bottle that was made of glass. She was enamored with it. She kept that bottle on her chest of drawers for a year. I told her several times that she just needed to throw that thing away. She fought me on it. I had Erin's mother and grandmother in the back of my mind. God was laying on my heart heavily to give them a gift that was the kids. I started making a pile for them, and that Dr. Pepper bottle was the first article that I placed there.

We moved over to her nightstand where her jewelry box and keepsake box were. I cleaned out her keepsake box and put those things in my bin. It was mainly souvenirs from the trips she had taken, ticket stubs from important places she visited, and letters that meant something to her. Her jewelry box wasn't but about eight inches tall. She got it in a yard sale and painted it. There wasn't much to it. It was a cheap little thing, but Erin refinished it herself, so it was the Mona Lisa. I don't know why Erin's maternal grandmother ran through my head then. God was working in me, and she needed something to remember her by. I decided to send her the jewelry box and a few other things from Peyton and Erin that did not have much monetary value, but were priceless. She would appreciate them.

The next thing we tackled was Erin's closet. I went through her dresses and accessories and kept the things that were important to me. There was a scarf that Erin wore everywhere she went. One of the most beautiful pictures of Erin was when she was wearing that scarf, standing with Radar's daughter, Tori. She needed to have this. It was something very special to Erin, and I couldn't think of a better place for it to be. Tori is also petite, so she got a few of Erin's clothes. Erin had gotten a new bedspread the week before she died. Sandy didn't want to keep it. So I decided to give that to Tori as well. Tori and Erin spent a lot of time together growing up. I knew she would appreciate these things.

As we were going through the closet, there was something that I was looking for. I had it flagged to be sent to her mom. It was Erin's cheerleader bag from middle school. Erin quit cheering because it interfered with soccer. She loved it, but she just loved soccer more and she had to make that choice. I have no idea how that would land on her mom, but I shipped it anyway.

I left one thing out of cleaning her room. This was a hard day, but I handled it pretty well until I came up on this one item. Erin loved her perfumes. She fell in love with a body spray from Bath & Body Works. I looked for it for several minutes before I found it. Isn't it weird how something you buy from a store can be your child? Every time I spray this body spray, I see Erin. It is weird how sometimes you know something will hurt and you almost welcome it. I keep that bottle of body spray in that bin along with all their other items that I either know I'm going to keep or I'm not sure. I do know though I have Erin in a bottle.

We donated most of Erin's clothes to the church's clothes closet. They were happy to get them because they said they mainly get out-of-date and out-of-style clothing. They're happy to get what they can get, but this was like a crown jewel to them. I am just glad that someone may get some enjoyment out of her clothes.

The day of cleaning out Erin's room was difficult. I don't think it was as bad as Peyton's, but nevertheless, it made for a hard day. I still have a lot of their items that are in storage that I have not gone through—things like Peyton's Hot Wheel cars and Erin's sewing machine. I'll keep the sewing machine because I'm going to learn how to sew one day.

Even though I walk through the darkest
valley, I will far no evil, for you are with me.

(PSALM 23:3–4 NIV)

Peyton Lives On

Jamal Anderson was a young man who was suffering from a liver disease. I really don't know much about his life and certainly didn't realize how his life was going to be a huge part of mine. We lived in the same community, but had no clue who each other was. On April 5, 2015, his liver disease was bringing him into the final stages of his life. He was brought to UAB Hospital to die. God answered a prayer for him the next day. Peyton was an organ donor. If you remember back to the beginning of the book, I told you all about Peyton's organ donation. Something went wrong with the confidentiality part of this process. I don't know if the news crews put two and two together. Maybe someone spoke who shouldn't have. I don't know. What I came to realize was that his family had been in the same waiting room as mine on April the 8th. The news crews jumped all over it. After all, it is a feel-good story that can show hope in tragedy. His sister was interviewed on television, and it became publicly known by the end of the day. I had so many other things to concentrate on that I could not deal with the emotions or physical settings of what was going on here. So many people in life love to try to put a positive spin on what is going on. That day showed me that there is a reason why you are not supposed to know the donor recipients. I couldn't deal with it. The burden of this was simply more than I could bear. When the soccer season continued, he was invited to that halftime tribute. I called the organ center to put a stop to it. It was just too soon. To be completely honest with you, I did everything in my power to put it out of my head. It was a good thing out of a bad thing, but it was also a daily reminder that my son was gone. He respected my wishes and never came to the game.

Christmas day 2015 was when God decided that it was time. Jamal contacted me out of the blue. We talked for a few minutes, and I had to ask one question. That question was: Why did you call? That young man said something to me that made me realize God was all in it. He told me that he was grateful to be alive and grateful for the blessings that God had bestowed on him. He also told me about the burden that God laid on his heart about me. He said that he knew that I was going through a tough time and he was simply calling to see what he could do to help. That day was both a struggle and a joy. God showed me the character of the young man who he needed to continue to live. The conversation that day was short and sweet. I figured that we only spoke for about fifteen to twenty minutes. It was on a day that I needed that reminder whether I wanted to hear it or not. That day, we decided to meet when I got back from my trip. It took us a couple of weeks to work out schedules and make this happen.

We met at a local barbecue restaurant for our first meeting. I'll never forget the first time I laid eyes on him. He's a very tall young man and walked in on a crutch. We greeted each other and began to talk. My first question that I asked him was about his crutch. I asked if this was a result of the liver transplant. He said no and that it was from wrecking his motorcycle. I immediately thought of his mother. I thought about how she probably was a nervous wreck. This young man had gotten a second chance at life and was making the most of it. I remember thinking that she probably wanted to put him inside a bubble for the rest of his life. If our roles were reversed, that is probably what I would do with Peyton. I was truly glad to see him doing well. God bestowed His gift on him. It seemed that he took this gift and continued on with life.

I had questions about his life—you know, about this disease, what happened to him, and the circumstances of his near demise. To be honest, I had to drag this out of him. This meeting was not about him. It was about helping me get through my side of it. That was his thought process. He really didn't have much to ask of me other than two questions. He wanted to know more about Peyton and Erin's death, and then he wanted to know how I was doing. That's it. There were no drama-filled conversations. There was nothing tongue in cheek that was said. It was all heartfelt and real. We had a great meeting. It lasted about an hour before we separated. The end of the conversation left me with two things. First, Jamal said, "My Italian intake has definitely increased after the transplant," and secondly, he had no intentions of this being the last time that we met.

You intended to harm me, but God intended
it for good to accomplish what is now
being done, the saving of many lives.

(GENESIS 50:20 NIV)

Blessings in Birmingham

I gave you a small taste of Jamal's character. Over the next couple of months, I became very curious of why God would bestow a gift upon him of this stature. Maybe God was putting it in my head, or maybe it was just me, but I had to see what has happened in his life that made this so real. To find out why God laid this on him, I would have to go where God's influence was the strongest. It took me a couple of weeks to set up to go to his church. I talked to his mother, and we got it all set.

Tracie and I went to Greater Mt. Carmel Missionary Baptist Church on a Sunday morning. I have to admit I was very nervous. I was driving into a high-crime unit. I had decided that God was in it and he would protect us. We walked into the church that morning. I don't know if Sunday school ran long or if we were just early. It was a quaint little church whose men and women were separated on either side doing their own respective lessons. When you cross ethnic boundaries, it makes you nervous. It took me just a second to realize that it wasn't reciprocated. One of the deacons approached us as we came in and simply asked if we were here to worship with them. He didn't care if I was White, purple, or pink with polka dots. His love for God shone through. Shortly after we got there, they disbursed their Sunday school meeting and started church. The senior pastor was away on assignment, and one of the junior pastors had stepped in. I was asked what brought us there, and I just responded by saying that we were guests of Marguriete (Jamal's mom) and Jamal. That was good enough for him. Marguriete came in a little bit late because Jamal wasn't feeling well and she needed to take care of him before she came. When she got there, she just came up beside me and asked me where her hug was. I stood up and gave her a big hug. She sat beside us, and we started worshipping together.

When you go into a church that is ethnically different from yours, you experience cultural differences that you don't see coming. The beginning of their service started with announcements and a little praise and worship. Then they came to recognition of visitors. All visitors were requested to stand and speak about themselves and tell why they were there. I was first. I remember standing and asking the congregation about the situation with Jamal needing a liver. I knew that they had to have all prayed for him many times over for healing. I then let them know that it was my son who lost his life and donated the liver to Jamal. I continued with saying, "I am here today because God blessed this church, and I needed to see what was so special about these people that God would bless them this much." The look on their faces were that of surprise and pain for my situation. Then it was like God covered everyone's hearts and love came back into play. We had a wonderful time in this church with these people. They went to extreme measures to make sure we were comfortable at all times.

That day, I spoke to many of Jamal's cousins, aunts, uncles, and of course the church grandma. There was even a moment that this book came up before it was even thought about. They saw it coming, and Tanya Parham made sure that I would get her name spelled correctly when I wrote it. It was just another way to cut tension and show us love in a lighthearted way.

The church service seemed to go on most of the afternoon, but it flew by. I met another side of my new family that day—a family placed in my life by God. I have not been back, but that is just simply because of time. Pastor Glaster (the senior pastor) has welcomed me back any time that I wish. I truly believe that it is not token. It is a genuine heartfelt request to stay in their lives.

I saw God's love that day. A love that shone through every one of those people. I believe they make God smile. If you ever make it out that way, please stop by this little church and tell them that this book brought you there. God favors this church, this I have no doubt, so God will bless you when you walk through those doors just as it did me. Thank you, Marguriete, and thank you, Pastor Glaster, along with the rest of this church for loving on me like you have. I am truly grateful.

Worship the Lord in the splendor of his
holiness. Tremble before him, all the earth.

(PSALM 96:9 NIV)

How to Pick a Good Fight

There have been a lot of events that you have read about that God was in. Now, I really want to take you along with me on the journey that God has led me through. Just to recap, God told me to be obedient to him and to fight with love. I have talked about a lot of the situations where I fought with love. Obedience has been sprinkled in as well.

A few years ago, God asked me to start a divorce class. It was sort of like this book. He gave me specifics to accomplish. The class was to be called Single Again. I followed his direction to a tee. When I handed it over to a church, it fell apart. It was a good learning tool for me. I have not gone anywhere with that class, but I learned a whole lot about one of the biggest crises in our world; that is divorce. I still have the information on my computer because I have a feeling that God would not get me to do something of that magnitude unless he needed the information to be used. Maybe it is this book or another I am to write? I don't know, but I'm prepared. My obedience to Him created Single Again. It has failed to this point in being what He needed it to be, but it was not a failure. He tested my obedience, and I did my best to fulfill that. I had no idea that my obedience would be tested to another level after the kids' deaths. Obedience is a weird thing. Every time that you feel that you have fulfilled what God has laid on you to do, it seems as if there's more to come. This last year has been filled with more to come.

Now I want to talk to you about something He put on my heart on obedience during my gauntlet. About three months after the kids' deaths, I finally understood what God was telling me to do. That is to seek him in many venues. I'm saying it this way because it took me a couple of weeks to figure out what that meant. Seek him in many venues. I was lost. What in the world is he asking me to do? He clarified for me later. I started visiting churches on Wednesday nights. I have gotten into a routine of coming to First Baptist Church of Athens every Sunday. I am enamored by the preacher there because it seems like God speaks straight through him to me. This left Wednesday nights open. My first task was to figure out where to visit, so I went to Facebook. My post was simple and pretty much straight to the point. I asked Facebook land where a good church would be to visit on a Wednesday night. I did not want to go to Bible studies or small groups. I wanted to be preached to. The first few times that this happened I got an overwhelming response. So here I go visiting churches of different denominations. The only requirement was what I stated earlier—that I wanted to be preached to. It didn't matter if it was a Church of Christ, Baptist, Church of God, Pentecostal, or any other church. I believe the first church that I went to was a nondenominational church. I believe it was just a warm up, but God sent me a message through it. The pastor there spoke about the devil. He went into pretty good detail about the devil. Through that sermon, one thing stood out to me. Lucifer was God's most powerful angel. Because he is so powerful and because of his own goals, he knows the Bible much better than any one of us. He is able to use scripture to get us off track, but the testimony that God has given us, he cannot refute. That's the message given to me on my very first mission to seek Him in many venues. God has given me a very powerful testimony that I hope He will use in His glory to destroy the evil against us. Can you imagine that being my first message? Wow, what a way to start. I don't believe that God gave me that message for any other reason than to get my attention.

God has given me other messages along the way. There have been a lot that were powerful, but it seems like most of them were like God was snapping his fingers at me and saying, "Hey, hey, pay attention!" Unfortunately, at the beginning, I didn't keep very good notes. It was more into the fall before I really started documenting. Most of my documentation is from the larger churches in the area. It seemed like I spent more time in the Baptist realm at the beginning. There were a lot of nondenominational churches that I visited as well, but they were basically the same beliefs as Baptist's. It wasn't very long before I started running out of places to go on a Wednesday night. You would be amazed of how many churches now use Wednesday night as a night to prepare for Sunday. They will do a lot of small groups and choir rehearsals instead of taking advantage of other ways to get God's message out.

So what do you do when seeking God in many venues has not run its course, but you're running out of venues to visit? What I did was recruit my best friend, a man that is very well versed in the Bible and has been a faithful warrior of God most of his life. You guessed it, God tapped Radar and, wow did he take it seriously. For the next several months, we were the dynamic duo visiting churches all over Birmingham. He researched and took this assignment to heart. I would sprinkle in places that I felt important to go to, but he was leading the charge. He took me deep into the realms of the Pentecostal faith as well as the Church of God faiths. I'm going to get into that, but I first want to tell you about God moving us to go to the Church of the Highlands.

I had gone to the Church of the Highlands once or twice before. Radar has never been, and God was placing on my heart to make sure I go this time. The first Wednesday of every month, Church of the Highlands brings in a high-powered speaker to give a message to the church. I had really enjoyed the previous services, but this one was going to change everything for me. Radar was not a big fan of going this night, but God was leading so we both were going to follow. When we got there, we went through praise and worship and then were informed that there would be no guest speaker. The pastor of the campus where we attended that night had a message for us.

What would you say to hearing a pastor who wanted to talk to us about picking a fight? It doesn't sound very godly, does it? And it doesn't sound like it would be a very good message. Trust me, guys, it was a good one. I'm going to give you the cliff notes version of this sermon, but it lasted for about an hour.

"How to pick a good fight." Supporting scriptures are Ephesians 6:11–12 (whole armor of God), 2 Chronicles 20:1, 2 Chronicles 19:14, and Matthew 20:28. If you want to pick a fight for God to battle for you, you have to first realize a couple of things. Our fight is with Satan and not people. The way we prepare and posture ourselves will ensure God's assistance. But how do we get God into the fight? The first way to get him into our fight is by making sure that we posture correctly. We have to have an other's first attitude. We have to do life with others and not do life alone. We have to remind ourselves of God's grace, and we have to depend on God. The pastor then encouraged us to read the Battle of Jehoshaphat in 2 Chronicles. Here Jehoshaphat was going into battle. He reminded God of his promise to him and that he would be victorious. God told Jehoshaphat how to prepare and posture himself. He told Jehoshaphat to put his praise and worship teams on the front line. When he did as God commanded, it seemed like they just called God to the battlefield. If you know the story, then you know that the armies that came against him that day turned against each other. Not one person in his army had to draw their sword.

Let there be no mistake. When you call God into action to fight on your behalf, not only will God come to your aid, but also it will provoke the enemy to attack. How do you get God to come to your aid? It is much easier than you think. All you have to do is what the Bible tells you to do anyway. There are three main parts to this battle plan. The first is random acts of kindness. If you see somebody that is truly struggling, whether it be a broken-down car on the side of the road or just crying in a church pew, a random act to help them for no reason other than to help them will make a huge difference. The second is service to others. Having an other's first attitude will give God glory and help His will to be done. And the third is to simply do His work in the community. Don't just sit in your pew on a Sunday morning. Be active. Ask what you can do to help. You may just get parking lot duty, or you may be asked to teach a Sunday school class. Whatever it will be, it will ensure God's intervention and anger the enemy. I promise you one thing, once you get God into it, the battle will be won before it begins just as it did with Jehoshaphat.

This works, guys. Satan has been after me to fall many times in my life. Since I have gotten God's battle plan, it has been an easier fight. I never realized how much sense this made. The beauty of this battle plan is that it makes you do exactly what you have been told to do from the beginning as a Christian when you come up on something bigger than what you can handle. Give it to God. What is different about this battle plan is that instead of handing it over and twiddling your thumbs, it commands you to be a Christian as Jesus intended. Love others as He loved you. If your focus is now on the stranded person on the side of the road, then you are not trying to take back what you have already given to God. You let Him fight it. Now, this provokes the enemy to attack, why? Well, that one is easy. The devil doesn't like to lose, so he will fight to the end. When he knows God is in it, he will push harder to try to get you to remove God. You know it's true. We falter in the face of evil way too much. We try to take it back over way too often. This battle plan helps you to concentrate on God even more. Who will lose? Who will win? Think it through.

Let's go back to seeking him in many venues. The main thing that I have learned is that each sin is different, but all sin is one. God sees it all as the same. I'm merely trying to show that seasoned Christians can be made to stumble simply by the rigidness of doctrine. Our own pride can maim or destroy the presence of God in others. I believe God needed me to see these things. He needed me to see how screwed up we are and how much we lean on our own understanding in our walks. I truly believe that this is making God sad. We are getting so caught up in the rules that we have missed the point. My God loves me. He wants to talk to me. He wants to hear from me every day. The days I don't talk to Him, I can just imagine how hurt He would be. There have been many people that have shared their hurt or worry because they haven't heard from me in a few days. God is the Creator, the Alpha, the Omega, and all He wants is a relationship. He allowed His son to be tortured and then killed so I could talk to Him, but yet we get so caught up in the rules. We get so caught up in our own understanding that we miss that very point. We are making each other stumble when all we need to do is be an example and lead people to Christ. Yeah, I'm going to fail. You're going to fail. We are all going to fail. There is no way we can be perfect. The only perfect one that has walked among us is Jesus. If we focus on our own paths instead of pointing out the flaws in someone else's paths, I am willing to bet that God's army would become much stronger. Furthermore, why are we trying to point out other people's flaws? It is up to the Holy Spirit to convict them of their sins. We have to figure out a way to put our differences aside and concentrate on the things we have in common. Most of all, we must do it in love. That is the only way to make God's army stronger. There are many people that may read this book and say that I am misguided. Their particular way is the only way. That is why God sent me to seek him in many venues. It is so that I can see the real damage that is being done to His people. I know God tells us to spread the good news so that people can be saved. I also know that there are some that are planters, some that are waterers, and some that are reapers. If you're not being watered, how can you water others? I submit to you the only way you can be watered is in your relationship with God.

The biggest thing that I learned through seeking God in many venues is that God honors faith and rewards obedience. How strong His presence was really depended on the service, not the church. Let that sink in for a second. What I learned was to look at what all of these churches had in common, not their differences. Now, I'm not the most fluent in scripture, but I believe that Jesus only got really angry once. He had table-flipping rage in the church (Luke 19:46). I feel like we are making church what we want it to be, not what God wants it to be. If you think about it, He never got mad at the people who did not know Him even after they persecuted Him and killed Him. He only got angry at us because we knew better.

The realization of fighting with love is a feeling that I really can't describe. It is a God thing. Talk to Him. You will receive it too.

Put on the full armor of God, so that you can
take your stand against the devil's schemes.

(EPHESIANS 6:11)

The Walk to Emmaus

I am coming up on the last of my firsts in my walk—one year since their deaths and one year from their funerals. It has been a rough ride. I have had breaks, but I feel destroyed. The pool of my blood by way of the thousands of paper cuts just fills my every thought, but the first year of my gauntlet was coming to an end, and I was excited to see it come in a weird way. After this, I knew what to expect, right?

Tracie had been wanting me to go on an Emmaus walk, but there just hadn't been a good time. I finally told her to just sign me up and God would work out the details. Boy, did he. I'll give you three guesses as to what weekend the walk fell on. Yep, you guessed it. I wound up going on the anniversary of Peyton's death. God cleared all of my schedule and made it happen. I know that there are people that have gone and had difficult experiences, but mine was wonderful. The Emmaus community is set up for a long weekend and is meant to be experienced with a closer relationship with God. It was a difficult weekend, but I need to tell you about it without giving away too much in case you decide to go on one yourself. The walk to Emmaus is in the Bible. When Jesus rose after the third day, he walked with two men on a road. They were headed to Emmaus. I believe that I have given you enough info to find where it is in the Bible, but I keep hearing my mentor saying that people are lazy and will not look it up for themselves. I need to give you a better reference. It is in Luke 24:13. He lifted the scales from their eyes so that these two men could see Him. This is the intent of what the New Covenant Emmaus Community is trying to achieve as well. But I already see God. So why would he want me to go? When you go through something like what I have, it makes you question everything. It just does. God has lifted me, and I have seen Him in so many ways. I have felt the Holy Spirit move through my very soul. But I still question him. I know that it didn't make sense, but God needed me to see Him. Along my journey earlier in the year, He spoke to me once. He told me that if I don't believe in Him, He will show me what we call coincidence. Yep, He removed all doubt. I spent Thursday night to Sunday night being pelted with coincidences. It was basically my walk over the last year with God all over again. Even after I thanked Him and told Him no further lesson was needed, He kept on coming. It was all about confirmation. Now, I saw God break strong men down to their knees that weekend. We cried at times like a bunch of babies. I would not take anything for it. I saw His power, and I needed to see just that. And guess how it started on Thursday night? The senior pastor, or spiritual leader as he was called, spoke to us about our differences in doctrine. He didn't point out specifics, but he told us to concentrate on the things we have in common, not those that separate us. We learned new songs as well as old ones and got some very good sermons throughout the weekend. Food was always at the ready with three meals served every day and snacks and drinks available at every location throughout the camp. When it was over, I felt like I had become a brother to sixteen other strangers. It was an amazing weekend. What a way to close my first year of the gauntlet of grief.

That is not the end though. On my way home about two weeks later, I'm talking with God. The big man takes me off of the bench and tells me to write this book. There were some unmistakable parts that I was told that made me know that it was from Him. I had told a lot of people that if I were tapped to write a book, then it would be named "Royal Peace," or the author would be Royal Peace (a name that was given to the kids after they had died and is now the name of my blog page on Facebook). God was very specific on the name, length, and author of this book, so I knew without a shadow of a doubt that it was Him. On top of this, He led me to write two speeches—one for youth and one for adults. I am not sure what the reason for the speeches are for. I figure that I will be speaking soon, but whatever God's plan is for me, I am obedient. He is confident in my abilities because they are His abilities. "Can't even walk without you holding my hand" (that is a beautiful Christian song by the way).

So I'm off. He has given me a plan, as well as direction, so here I go. This one will go without a flaw now, right? (Do you remember the divorce class?) Um, no. It has been a struggle. Distractions started coming from everywhere—small distractions, but nevertheless, hurdles to jump. Work started getting busy in the slow time of their year; extra jobs that friends needed my help with came to the front burner; both of my vehicles started giving me problems, all at the same time. Let's just say it started slow and rocky. Oh yeah, I was asked to work a Chrysalis Walk, too (that is an Emmaus Walk for youth). It's okay though; God is in control, so it will work itself out.

Radar continually tells me that I give Satan more credit than he deserves. That objective criticism makes me think every time I come up against something like this. Was it the devil that was throwing obstacles, or was God doing it to keep my eyes on Him? To be honest, Jesus and I will have a talk about that one day in heaven. Until then, I will just thank God every time he talks to me and leads my path.

About a month into it, I got writer's block. I just had no direction on what I was going to write about next. So I switched gears and wrote the speeches. They are different and just hit the highlights of this book, but it is what God needed to get me back on the right path. This put me behind though because I spent too much time on the speeches. My friends are saints. I started getting irritated because I was feeling the pressure of the deadline. They took a beating and neglect. Why? Because I'm trying to take over again. I'm trying to be

His servant and forgot all about being His friend. About two weeks before the deadline, I went to the altar. I hit my knees and prayed. Lord, have mercy on me. I have failed you again. I can't seem to get out of your way.

God answered my prayer before I got the prayer completely spoken. I had not passed my deadline yet, but I knew that I could not make it. His response still tickles me a little. He has fun with different mannerisms with me. One day, He talks to me in almost an old English, or king's English form, and other times, it's normal. Then He will sometimes talk to me in slang vernacular. This particular time, it was almost a Larry the Cable Guy terminology. He said, "That's okay, buddy. Just get it done." And people don't think God has a sense of humor. He needed me to smile. He doesn't want me to concentrate on failing Him; He wants to walk with me. If I run late writing my book, then He is God; He can fix it. If I'm goofing off with the boss, He will change the timetable. Or was it changed and known before it happened? Master of time and owner of prophecy He is, just like Master Yoda, but for real.

Okay, okay, okay. Back to it. On the deadline, things started falling apart again. I don't know why, but God and I are doing our thing. My friends are helping. I'm hitting on all cylinders and am really moving through this. This time, it is a little bit bigger stuff though, and it is coming up on Father's Day. I don't know, again, whether it was the devil or God. I just know I was getting hit from all angles. After about a week of it, I hit my knees and Facebook to enlist some prayer warriors. You know, He can be like superman sometimes. After I got the power of prayer going, He sent the messages I needed to finish this book. The last two chapters were here. Don't get me wrong, Father's Day was miserable, as I expected, but I had friends to help me through it. If you are reading this today, then God saw this through and is showing His love for us both in every word.

Then will the eyes of the blind be opened
and the ears of the deaf unstopped.

(ISAIAH 35:5)

The Sine of Bell

I want to go back to something that Robert told me during a counseling session. I know enough psychology to be dangerous. I was given another one of those "grief charts" the other day. It was by someone who had suffered great loss as I have and had great intentions. I want to make something clear. My irritation is with the psychology community. It is not with people that are trying to share something that may help someone else as it did them. I have to admit that the grief chart was well thought-out and had twenty-two points of grief indicators in it. The problem with charts like this, especially ones with bell curves, suggests that a cycle can be completed. As well-meaning as these charts may be, they suggest a farce. They suggest that you can go through something of this magnitude and there will be a finality to it. This is far from the truth. What has happened to me has changed my very existence. Life as I knew it is gone. That doesn't necessarily mean that that is a negative thing. With change comes adaptation. Most of the people in the psychology world know this and take it for granted that everyone knows it. I'm going to dive into this chart for a moment. I have dissected the points to this chart into two categories. One is raw emotion, while the other is behavior.

Raw emotions such as shock, numbness, anger, fear, panic, guilt, loneliness, and depression are the result of going through a traumatic experience. Specifically, what irritates me with charts of this nature is the fact that you cannot single out any one of these things. I live with every one of these emotions simultaneously every day. Some become more prevalent than others and rise to the surface. But let there be no mistake, they are all there. I felt a portion of these emotions when the kids died. All of these emotions overtake my very being. If you choose to try to chart something of this nature, a bell curve does not do it justice. You need to look at it as more of a sine wave that floats up and down on a timeline. I believe these raw emotions are exactly what allows you to make poor choices during your stages of grief. It also makes me understand why unhealthy habits such as drug, alcohol, and many other addictions come into play. Trying to chart the stages of grief is flawed from the very beginning. The reason why it's flawed is because of the direction that it was started. I'm sure if you have taken a psychology class, you have heard the four stages of grief. It has now grown into seven primary stages. When this precept was originally introduced, it was to explain what a person would go through when faced with their own mortality, such as a terminal illness. There is a finality there. Here there is not. Trying to transform that thought process has its difficulties, and I believe is ineffective.

The primary difference between the two subjects is that one is dealing with what is about to happen where the other is dealing with what has happened. When you deal with aftermath, none of the pieces that you pick up are whole. Fragments sometimes cannot be repaired. I believe this is why it invokes all of the emotions almost simultaneously. As you're able to deal with certain parts of these raw emotions, life can get a little bit better. That is when another fragment hits you and you fall once again. I call this a paper cut. They are triggered by pictures, smells, memories, and many other things. So many people are given hope in thinking that if you go through this cycle, then you can complete this stage. I believe that how you have dealt with one aspect of these emotions contributes to how quickly you bounce back. The problem is that you're defensive. There is nothing to attack, so you have to wait on these emotions to surface.

When they surface, you can then start to deal with them. The biggest problem in this battle is the fight-or-flight thought process. When you're in panic mode and it's something bigger than you, this mode will hit you. It's the determining point of how you're going to deal with the situation at hand. If you decide flight, you can run. You can dive into a bottle or jab a vein. It's that simple. The problem comes in with finality. There is none here. This means that it will be waiting for you when you come back or when you sober up. This monster can wait until the end of time. I had a pretty good grip on this understanding when this happened to me. The analogy that I used to my counselor was a brick wall. I cannot come to the wall. I have to wait for the wall to come to me. I know that doesn't make sense, but the wall was not the situation. It is the emotions that surface. You can rush to the wall and try to break it down all you want; the fact is that the emotions will come out in their own time. You can't rush them, and you cannot run from them. Sometime in your life, you're going to have to deal with it. The choice of dealing with the emotions will come in their own time. You can't control it. I think this is the problem with the charts. It's very easy to look back and see that you have dealt with these categories. It is easy to pick them out of a list. I can remember back in the first month where I experienced every one of these emotions simultaneously.

The second category that I want to talk about is behavior in loss adjustment. They are usually the result of how you deal with your raw emotions. There are many charts that mix these. I believe, though, in the theories of cause and effect. First, I need to give you a sample list of the behaviors that I'm talking about on this chart. They are denial, emotional outbursts, searching, disorganization, isolation, reentry troubles, new relationships, new strengths, new patterns, hope, affirmation, and helping others. These behaviors were listed and scattered through the chart that I was given. Now some may want to pick parts out to argue, but just hold on a second. These parts are the primary ones that I will discuss. Denial is the first monster that I want to tackle and one of the hardest for me to overcome. We try to make things very complex, but there is one simple fact: when you try to run from your emotions or hide from them, you get this 800-pound gorilla. Denial is a hard pill to break down but is so easy and natural to do. In my grief process, I had to face this battle many times just in my first year alone. I would wind up going to the other extreme of talking about the kids' deaths daily, which would slam me into many of those other emotions. At the beginning, it seemed like the more I talked about the kids, the worse my depression and anxiety got. I am a head-on-type person though. I have not run from many things in my life.

Isolation was a behavior that I practiced the most. Part of it was a result of denial. Part of it was a result of searching. The funny thing about my isolation is that I would do it in public. Walmart was my choice of places. It might amaze you to know that I have walked miles inside of Walmart without speaking to a soul. It was a way for me to be social without actually having to be social. I would run through all of these emotions in my head as I walked, and I am willing to bet that there are some security guards, Walmart employees, and customers that probably think I'm not playing with a full deck. Thinking back on it now, I'm betting that a sporting goods store would have been a better choice. Whenever I would experience anger, I could have just migrated to the boxing equipment. When I experienced frustration, the golf simulator probably would have taken a beating. The fact is, though, that I wound up spending many, many hours in my car in the parking lot. I'm not saying by any means that my way was correct, but if you have dealt with similar things, then you understand why.

There was a behavior on this list that surprised me a little. That behavior is hope. I get it, but most in my position would not. What is there to hope for? I believe that hope is the acknowledgment of these emotions and desire for something more than what they have in their life at this point. That's really easy to say as well as self-explanatory, but when you are in the monster of depression, it feels unattainable. Unfortunately, hope could be the very thing that would spiral you downward all over again. It's not for having hope alone, it is more for what you hope for. Once you can truly accept what is happening to you, then you can move forward.

I bet you're wondering why I took this left turn into the psychology world. It is basically because we are trying to use our own understanding to figure out what is happening to us. God continually tells us not to do this, but we can't help it. We do it anyway. So if we're going to do it, let's dive a little deeper into it then. There is an accepted theory in the psychology world from the 1980s. It is called the elaboration likelihood model or ELM. Basically, this theory is about persuasion and how this persuasion affects us in changing our behaviors. I don't care to go too deep into the definition of this model, but I believe that it helps explain what is going on. You don't want to hurt. You don't want to cry. You don't want to feel the pain and the loss that is happening to you. Moreover, your friends and family don't want you to experience it either. It is very easy for them to persuade you out of this, and it is even easier to persuade yourself. I believe this is why we hang on to charts, graphs, and inspirational messages. You can't seem to understand that you need this pain to truly move beyond it and to help better yourself and your life. I don't want you to misinterpret what I'm saying. This will change your life. It has mine. The life that I am living seems alternate just because I thought it would go a different way. The psychology world calls it a "new normal." Man, I hate that term. I hate everything that it stands for. It angers me to even hear it being classified. It is called a new normal because we have expectations—we have desires. A life event takes place and changes how we feel our life should go. So many times in life, we can't even see what's going on before our very eyes, so we persuade ourselves. We hurt and we cry and we scream it's not fair. I have been given a hand that I don't want to play. I don't think anybody wants to play it, but I have no choice. If you choose to rely on earthly understandings or are struggling between the two on the subject of why me—why is this happening—please take that persuasion model and apply it to a different realm. What is the devil persuading you to do? What is God persuading you to do? This is an argument that I choose not to be a part of. Let God sort it out. I'll debate Jesus on it while we're watching the kids play soccer in heaven.

STAGES OF GRIEF

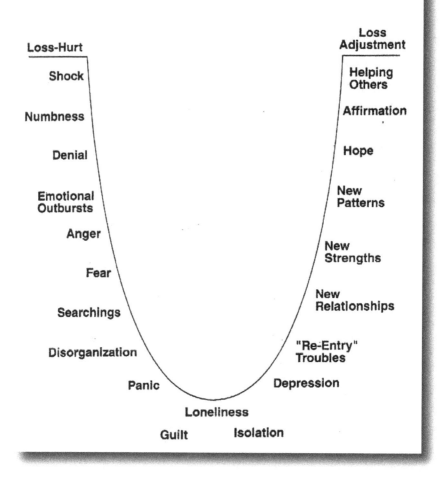

Loss-Hurt
Shock
Numbness
Denial
Emotional Outbursts
Anger
Fear
Searchings
Disorganization
Panic
Guilt
Loneliness
Isolation
Depression
"Re-Entry" Troubles
New Relationships
New Strengths
New Patterns
Hope
Affirmation
Helping Others
Loss Adjustment

Trust in the Lord with all of your heart and
lean not on your own understanding.

(PROVERBS 3:5 NIV)

God's Little Gift

I love you—each and every one of you. I understand so much
more about the concept of love. It has touched me at the deepest
level during the last year. I don't think I could ever comprehend
it until now. There are many of you that I don't like, but I still love
you. It's what Jesus commands, and it is what I try to show. In love,
we can do so many things that represent hate. Sometimes it's hard to
distinguish between the two even though they are set as opposites.
There is not a day that goes by that I don't want to isolate myself. I
want to crawl in a hole. There is a reason why I'm here. Maybe it's
this book? Maybe God has many more things in store for me? I don't
know. All I can do is to start with love.

I am now starting my second year of my gauntlet of grief. The
things you have read about have all happened in one year's time. The
year seemed long, but in other areas, it seemed like a blink of an eye.
God was in it though. As I was in church this morning, the pastor
talked about how God uses us when we're broken. He has to allow us
to break before His will can be done through us. I completely get it. I
pray that I am doing His will because you are reading this book today.
But I want to step out for a second and tell you about the next process

that this book is about to go through. God laid it on my heart to write this book. He didn't lay it on my heart to edit it nor publish it. He has placed a lady in my life to edit the book. I have seen her from time to time in this church. She is a very nice lady and very well respected in the community. All I knew was that she was a retired professor at a local university. God tapped her. When I went to let her know that God had tapped her, I learned a little bit more about her. Her background is not important, but let there be no mistake, God has more than qualified her for this task. The thing that you need to see is that God sees her. I didn't know this woman unless you want to count passing her in the hallways and her stopping to say she's praying for me. It's not important that I know her. It's not about my understanding. God sees her. God told me to come to her and use her for His glory. When I spoke to her in this conversation, she never hesitated. She is following His will too. I know that. The editor of this book doesn't have to worry if she is a child of God. If someone asks her, there are people that can answer the question for her. Does God see me? Am I a child of God? I hope that someone can answer yes for me in the same way. The real question is, can God see you? Because if He can see you, He will use you. Don't get me wrong; He can see you, but just has not used you yet. That may be why you're going through this pain. It's coming. All you have to do is to love Him more than yourself. It is the only way you're going to get through this.

In the last chapter, we got deep into the psychology world. I brought up a lot of things that we use to lean on our own understanding. There is something here though that we have to talk about. If you're not in the right place when something like this hits you, then you have an even larger battle to fight. I have met several people that could not cope with life before they were hit with something of this magnitude. Some may have already been on medications to help deal with daily struggles. Their starting point was behind mine. By the same token, there have been others that did not have nearly the battle to fight because of how deeply rooted they were in God. I get it. I completely understand how you feel like you would commit suicide or become an addict of some form. I also understand how easy it is to go to a doctor and let them give you medication so you can't feel it. Because we are fighting the hardest fight of our lives, I would like to pray with you for a second.

Dear Heavenly Father, we come today just to thank you and praise you for everything you do for us. Please cover this person in your blanket of love and grace. The struggle that is ahead of them is so great that they cannot do it alone. Please grab them up and reveal yourself to them so that you can make their path straight as you have mine. We need you, and we love you. Please place us in favor and keep us in favor as we go through our gauntlets of grief. With all these things, in Christ's name I pray. Amen.

Our walks are not for the faint of heart. God has allowed us to go through this because we are strong. If you don't believe that, then there is strength within you that you have not tapped into yet. There is a special little gift inside your heart that God has given you. Maybe you need to search there? God left it for you. You just have to find it. If you need a clue, his name is Jesus. He's not going to forsake you. In fact, He's going to place things in your life that will show you what you're capable of. All you have to do is to realize one thing. If you don't believe in God, He will show you coincidence.

If you are a support person and are reading this book to try to figure out how to help a dear friend or family member, let me pray with you.

Dear Heavenly Father, as we come again today, we thank you and praise you for everything you've done for us. We are grateful for the day that you have made and grateful for the love that you have given us to try to help others. We realize that nothing of this earth can give our friend or family member that which only you can bestow on us. Please give us wisdom, strength, and patience to help guide them back to you. As we are reminded by scripture, we know that the power of prayer is the most lethal weapon in your arson. Help us be reminded that by talking to you daily, we can only then be of true service. Please place us in favor and keep us in favor as we support your child. With all these things, in Christ's name I pray. Amen.

Either way, I pray this book finds you well. I hope that something in it can help you find real peace. I pray that something here might help you move forward. Regardless of your circumstance, death brings us all to the same plane, and we can only survive it with our Savior. Fight with love.

For God so loved the world that he gave his
one and only son that whoever believes in
him shall not perish but have eternal life.

(JOHN 3:16 NIV)

About the Author

C hris Spain was born and raised in Birmingham, Alabama. After becoming a single dad, he began to realize that he was not able to control his circumstances. He had to look to God to lead him. He raised his children to do the same. He is not a priest, a preacher, or an elder in the church. He is merely a broken shell of a man that has survived a tragedy.

Printed in the USA
CPSIA information can be obtained
at www.ICGtesting.com
LVHW022317230823
756079LV00010B/168